RECONCILING OUR DIFFERENCES

*A Christian approach to recognising
Aboriginal Land Rights*

RECONCILING OUR DIFFERENCES

A Christian approach to recognising Aboriginal Land Rights

FRANK BRENNAN S.J. (ed.)

AURORA BOOKS

DAVID LOVELL PUBLISHING

First published in 1992 by
Aurora Books
an imprint of Jesuit Publications
300 Victoria Street
Richmond, Victoria 3121

in association with
David Lovell Publishing
308 Victoria Street
Brunswick, Victoria 3056

Cover photo: Jeffery Miller from Yarrabah, Qld
    and Kris Dwaard from Edmonton, Qld
Cover design by Stanley Wong
Typeset in 11.5/13 Times by Jesuit Publications

National Library of Australia
Cataloguing-in-Publication data

Reconciling our differences : a Christian approach to recognising
    Aboriginal land rights.

ISBN 1 86355 030 5.

[1] Aborigines, Australian – Land tenure.   2. Land tenure –
Australia – Religious aspects – Catholic Church.   I. Brennan,
Frank, 1954–   .

333.20994

Foreword

PATRICK DODSON
Chairperson, Council for Aboriginal Reconciliation

At the 1967 constitutional referendum, the Australian nation as a whole stood up to be counted. Those eligible to vote stood up and declared themselves for basic recognition and common decency. They stood up for Aboriginal and Torres Islander peoples' rights as members of the Commonwealth of Australia.

Again the nation as a whole is being asked to stand up and be counted. We have been given a challenge, and an opportunity as a nation, to recreate the common view of 1967, to seek common ground, and to recognise our common nationhood. I believe it to be our one chance.

The Council for Aboriginal Reconciliation has formulated a vision for its task leading up to the centenary of federation in 2001. We reached this common vision despite our differences and our prejudices, despite the hostility and separatism that has entered into Aboriginal affairs.

The council's vision is for a united Australia which respects this land of ours, values the Aboriginal and Torres Strait Islander heritage and provides justice and equity for all. Our goal is to have the nation share this vision by the year 2001. The challenge for the nation is to work at making this vision a reality. We will need to make the time available so that we can sit down together, black and white, and work for a common approach. The first step will be to concentrate upon the nature and quality of our relationship with each other.

In the past, that relationship was based on the perceived need for Aborigines to change their ways. Now Aboriginal and Torres Strait Islander people are asking other Australians to change their ways, their attitudes, their laws and their daily practices. Like the river meeting the ocean, we can merge without losing our own identity.

Australia is now one nation of many peoples. We share a commonwealth of interests and aspirations. We are yet to find our national spirit—the spirit that would allow us all to belong comfortably together in one place, talking together about our shared and different hopes, aspirations and needs. That search cannot be sidetracked by arguments over money and power, by pushing one-sided agendas, or by not being willing to have dialogue and interaction.

The Council for Aboriginal Reconciliation cannot do this for people. People have to do it for themselves. We have to work together for change. I welcome this contribution to the reconciliation process by the Jesuits of Australia. Reconciliation cannot proceed without recognition and justice for all parties. These essays by theologians and other experts in their fields should assist Australians of goodwill to come to terms with our history and to commit themselves to a better future for all citizens in the playgrounds, on the streets, and in the workplaces throughout this land.

Governments have a role in this, but we cannot wait for governments to reconcile our differences. The job of reconciliation, co-operation, and communication has to be taken on by all individuals and groups in society. That is the challenge to the nation and to our national identity. As Mr Wenten Rubuntja, a member of the Council for Aboriginal Reconciliation, said at the time of the Barunga Statement in 1988:

> Today, there are lots of people living in this country. People who have come from all over the world. But we don't call them

foreigners. We don't ask, 'Where's your country? Where's your father from?' They have been born here. Their mother's blood is in this country ... This is their country too now.

So all of us have to live together. We have to look after each other. We have to share this country. And this means respecting each other's laws and culture.

I hope that in the year 2001 we can celebrate our common vision as Australians, reconciled to each other and our history.

Contents

Introduction

FRANK BRENNAN SJ

Some differences between people are based on respect for the other's culture, dignity and rights. These differences need to be recognised and affirmed. Other differences between people arise from individual actions and even a national history of discrimination and injustice. These differences need to be overcome by change of heart, mindset, laws and social policies. Reconciliation between Australia's indigenous people and the migrants and their descendants requires personal commitment and changes to laws and policies which have driven a wedge between us for so long. We need to become more comfortable with the differences which enhance our lives and cultures, while overcoming the differences which separate us and do violence to our lives and cultures. Reconciliation is both a national task and a personal commitment.

Talk of an Aboriginal treaty has been around for years. Often it highlights the anger of Aborigines and the fear of other Australians. The music of Yothu Yindi has brought it strikingly into the Australian consciousness. Yet, 204 years after Governor Phillip's arrival at Sydney Cove, no one quite knows what such a legal document would look like.

During the bicentenary, Prime Minister Hawke signed the Barunga Statement with two Aboriginal leaders, committing his government to the negotiation of a treaty. One of those leaders, Mr Galarrwuy Yunupingu, said, 'There should be one Australia and we should be part of it. But our part should be on our terms.' The federal opposition pledged to tear up any document on the basis that a treaty, being technically an agreement between two sovereign nation states, would be an inappropriate agreement between Aborigines and others when all members of both parties were citizens of Australia, an independent sovereign nation. Though the Fraser government had been prepared to negotiate an agreement with Aborigines, the coalition when in opposition has claimed to be more concerned with substantive contribution to Aboriginal welfare rather than symbolism acknowledging the place of Aborigines in contemporary Australia. There is a need for both.

The first centenary of the Australian Constitution, 1 January 2001, is an appropriate target date for finalising arrangements recognising Aboriginal entitlements. Being responsible for shaping a new future under the rule of law, we have to own our past as a nation and make up for the shortfall, dispossession and disadvantage suffered by Aborigines for eight generations. In the historic *Mabo* decision handed down on 3 June 1992, the High Court of Australia has exploded the myth of *terra nullius*. But two centuries of dispossession preceded the decision. As a matter of legal theory, Aborigines, having been dispossessed, were included among the people who, 'relying on the blessing of Almighty God', on 1 January 1901 agreed to unite in an indissoluble Commonwealth of Australia. There never was such an agreement. On 27 May 1992, we celebrated the twenty-fifth anniversary of the referendum which removed the two adverse references to Aborigines from the Constitution. Our Constitution now does not mention Aborigines. It does not protect their rights as the indigenous people of the continent. Neither does our legal system guarantee Aborigines the right of self-determination within the nation. Now is the time to negotiate such an agreement. The High Court has set right the law of the land; we still need to set right the law for living together, respecting each other's law and culture.

The commonwealth parliament has now unanimously voted for legislation setting up the Council for Aboriginal Reconciliation which has a decade to investigate the desirability of an 'instrument of reconciliation'. Many Aborigines are understandably dubious in light of the Hawke government's abandonment of national land rights and word games about treaties, compacts and instruments of reconciliation. The council's chairperson, Mr Patrick Dodson, says, 'The goal of reconciliation, coming after 200 years of violence and division, needs all the support it can get.' Some, including Mr Michael Mansell and his Aboriginal Provisional Government, claim separate nation status and will not be party to any domestic Australian agreement. Expecting Mansell and Dodson to agree on an instrument of reconciliation is as unreal as expecting Mr Keating and Dr Hewson to agree on the flag. In each case, there has at some appropriate time to be a determination of what the majority of those affected are seeking. Even in the absence of unanimous support, the justifiability and achievability of those goals must then be assessed.

Even if the day were approaching when social indicators revealed that Aborigines as a group were no longer poor, disadvantaged and dispossessed, we would still need to consider the issue of indigenous rights. Aborigines should not be forced to be migrants in their own land. They should be able to preserve their own culture, laws and social organisation provided they do not interfere with the rights and liberties of others and provided their communities guarantee individuals a freedom to opt into mainstream Australian life with its benefits and disadvantages.

The twelfth of October 1992 marked the 500th anniversary of Columbus's discovery of the Americas and the commencement of the International Year for the World's Indigenous Peoples with the theme 'Indigenous Peoples—A New Partnership'. In the decade ahead, the Constitutional Centenary Foundation chaired by Sir Ninian Stephen will consider proposals for constitutional reform in Australia. The constitutional recognition of indigenous rights is being considered. The High Court's *Mabo* decision makes it clear that Aboriginal land title survives and is legally enforceable under our law in areas where the crown has not validly created new property rights in the land. All parties now need to come to the table to negotiate and effect the compromises necessary so that we all may own the social institutions for the resolution of conflict, knowing that every Australian's place is strong in this land.

In 1985 and 1986, we Australian Jesuits produced two editions of *Finding Common Ground*[1] which assessed the moral and scriptural bases of land rights. The renewed calls for recognition of indigenous rights and reconciliation prompt us to write again as a group of Jesuits wanting to contribute to the resolution of outstanding claims in Australian society. Informed by the Christian tradition, we offer these reflections on the process and outcome of reconciliation. John Eddy, Senior Research Fellow at the Australian National University, outlines the history of race relations in this land. Brian McCoy, researcher with the Royal Commission into Aboriginal Deaths in Custody, demonstrates the link between that history and the contemporary reality of poverty, disadvantage and dispossession. I then trace the path in legal theory from *terra nullius* to constitutional recognition of Aboriginal rights. Moral theologian William Daniel explores the limits of self-determination. Systematic theologian John Wilcken and scripture scholar Brendan Byrne provide theological and scriptural approaches to reconciliation. The appendices comprise the Pope's speech at Alice Springs in 1986 and the Catholic Bishops' 1990 Pastoral Letter on reconciliation. Strong and informed in our own traditions and cultures, we should be able to live together in this land.

Chapter 1

Recognition, Reconciliation and History

JOHN J EDDY SJ

'But the past is still alive, is dangerously alive, in many parts of Australia',
Henry Reynolds in *Frontier* (Sydney, 1987, p. ix).

Leopold von Ranke set historians an impossible goal, forever beyond human grasp, when he exhorted them to find out *wie es eigentlich gewesen ist*—what really happened, or, literally, how it really was. But he also, as Barbara Tuchman notes, found 'the truth more interesting and beautiful than the romance', and she writes that even though we who investigate the past were not there and can never be certain that we have recaptured it as it really was, 'the least we can do is to stay within the evidence'.[1]

The cynic might judge that most people find coping with present events and necessary practical decisions for the immediate future sufficient burden. It is hard enough to grasp essential daily details, and summon up enough courage to survive. An interest in the past may be a fine hobby, but contributes little that is useful or helpful. This is to ignore the role of memory and reflection in human life. History is the memory of an individual or community, the story of its identity, and how it became what it now is and can hope to be. Without history there can be no understanding of the present and future, no

vision and no judgement. It is true that we can hope only to
come to a conditioned and limited recognition of our past, and
that memory can play tricks and be abused. It is also clear that
history cannot be recycled, though, as George Santayana pointed
out, those who ignore the mistakes of the past are often doomed
to repeat them. Truth may be difficult to ascertain, and unpleasant to face once discovered, but without it there can be no
firm foundation, and, in St John's searing words, 'the truth will
make you free'.[2]

The story of nations, as of individuals, is full of themes,
events and attitudes—all of which arise from the human condition, and some of which deeply affect the essential characteristics and very identity of the subject. Australian history is no
exception, and no area is more sensitive or more in need of
recognition and reconciliation than that of 'racial' relations,
the original and ongoing 'conversation' between black and
white. In the aftermath of the *Mabo* decision in the High Court,
there may be a temptation for the majority of Australians to
drive on, ignoring the past and the communal memory, and
simply treat the Aboriginal minority as one small if significant
group of Australians, not especially entitled to any privileges
or warranting any exceptional attention. 'Many white Australians certainly believe', wrote Henry Reynolds in anticipation
of the Bicentenary of 1988, 'that the legal, political and moral
issues in the land rights campaign will fade away if people stop
brooding about the past and if more money is spent'—on
education, health, housing and so on. But this, he rightly
predicted, would not touch 'the heart of the matter'. As is its
wont, a great weight of history, of ancient injustice, lost land
and martyred kin, presses the cause forward and will not be
denied.[3]

History itself is no dry-as-dust activity, and can claim no
finality or infallibility even where there exists general consen-
sus. Like politics or law it can become a battleground, especially when it discloses conflict or injustice which still festers,
creates guilt and cries out for redress. It is customary, and

correct, for historians to confess their limitations and suscepti-
bility to bias. As Peter Biskup remarks, historians do not exist
in a vacuum and cannot be expected to transcend the values of
their times. In such a delicate area as white-black relations it
would be doubly unfair if white historians maintained a monopoly, and even for those sincerely seeking reconciliation
there are pitfalls. When John Molony wrote his introduction to
the Penguin *Bicentennial History of Australia*, he spoke evoca-
tively of the black people 'glimpsed fleetingly in these pages'
and felt it was not his 'privilege to write their history'. He
thought it was 'not for me or any new Australian to beg those
who were here, who were at one with their land for so long
before us, to join now in being one people'; but he sought some
sense of reconciliation as 'our first aspiration'. In protest at the
European nature of the Bicentennial celebrations, his book was
thrown into Sydney Harbour.[4]

     Yet, as Gandhi said, the road to the future lies over the
bones of the past, on which we dare to tread, and each must do
what can be done. In his *Sharing the Country*, Frank Brennan
notes: 'I am not an Aborigine and I do not presume to speak for
Aborigines. I am a white Australian who seeks greater reconciliation with the descendants of the traditional owners of this
land—a reconciliation based on justice for all Australians,
including the descendants and inheritors of those who dispossessed Aborigines and the most recently arrived migrants and
refugees who have done no wrong to Aborigines'. Those
historians, most of them white and most of them working
within the last twenty-five years, who have radically revised
the record of our past may not have told the whole story of
white-black relations yet, but they deserve great credit for
recognising and relating truths which have been neglected,
covered over or denied (what Frank Brennan calls 'unfinished
business'), and for giving as much voice as possible to the
Aboriginal presence, variety, richness and humanity which
must form part of the understanding of reconciled Australia.
     Since the 1960s there has been an explosion in Aborigi-

nal history. Biskup provides a critical review of the beginnings in the first chapter of *New History*.[5] Sophisticated and well-attended courses are offered in many tertiary institutions, and the field's high standards are evident in *Aboriginal History*, the pages of which periodical, founded in 1977, give abundant witness to the expertise and professionalism of this 'specialist' area of history. All this new knowledge may not of itself bring about wisdom in either theory or practice, and learning can be marshalled to support unworthy causes. Even the brilliant Baldwin Spencer, with his acute grasp of Aboriginal ways and capacity to lead the field, accepted a Frazerian framework and deemed the European to be of a 'higher form' of humanity.[6]

Max Charlesworth, in his introduction to *Religion in Aboriginal Australia* (Brisbane, 1984), gives testimony to the revolution in Aboriginal studies which was heralded by the work of C.D. Rowley, W.E.H. Stanner and others. In such a central field as the study of religion, he remarks on the 'melancholy mixture of neglect, condescension and misunderstanding' which had preceded the 1950s, and the 'atmosphere of general neglect, distortion, misunderstanding and trivialisation' that prevailed before due respect was given to the uniqueness and richness of Aboriginal spirituality and its importance for the broader understanding of the Australian experience in its spiritual dimension.[7]

At almost every level, there have been massive revisions and re-interpretations of our history as it affects the Aborigines over the last 30 years, and much is now agreed. Many areas of popular misunderstanding, ignorance and prejudice have been at last 'corrected', although much remains to be examined and the results communicated to a wider public in the necessary and healing task of recognition and reconciliation. In the new climate Aboriginal voices are welcomed and respected: the subject after all centres on their past and the memory of it.

When the First Fleet arrived in 1788, closely shadowed by the rival French, there was about to take place a series of events from which flowed the foundation of white Australia as we know it, and nothing short of a catastrophe for the original inhabitants. The ingredients of conflict were there from the first. Indeed the nature of the penal settlement itself has given rise to rival views. Earlier European contacts had not prepared the convict settlers and their guardians for their first or continuing relations with the Aborigines. The convicts, as revisionist historians have pointed out, were not necessarily vitiated representatives of a 'criminal class'. Nor were they the worst 'human capital' that could have been devoted to founding a new society in the Antipodes. But evidence suggests that their tainted legal, social and economic status, and the consequent air of penal discipline and official insistence on the maintenance of 'order', had a tragic role in shaping relations with the indigenous peoples.[8]

The British nation was, as Noel Butlin and others have pointed out, in 'crisis mode' from the Industrial Revolution onwards. Each phase which—from the first days until now—made the United Kingdom the main source of white migrants to Australia had its impact, and each generation experienced new tensions and challenges. Settlement spread 'as ink spreads on blotting paper'. Caught off-balance in various places and in different ways and at varying paces, the Aborigines reacted to the whites in a complex way. The result throughout the continent was often roughly similar, but each regional, personal and communal subtlety and specificity has still to be recognised and appreciated. The past lives on and, although we may agree with Stanner that it is the *now* that counts, that now 'has a history from which it is inseparable if it is to remain comprehensible'.[9]

The alarming limitations of our knowledge are illustrated even by the sketchy nature of the available demographic facts. There is still debate about the numbers of Aborigines living in 1788. The older estimate of about 250,000 seems to be short of the mark, while Noel Butlin's early extrapolation of approximately a million appears to be too high. The best estimates now settle for perhaps three quarters of a million. It is an important question, for it is now accepted that the Aborigines formed the majority of the inhabitants of Australia, despite the depredations of disease and displacement, until well after it was imagined and asserted that they were 'dying out'. Another sad gap concerns our lack of certainty about the eventual balance sheet of the casualties of violence consequent on white settlement. Again the best current estimates are about 3000 for the whites and perhaps ten times as many, and certainly over 20,000, for the Aborigines.[10]

Successive periods of Australian settlement, each dominated by new social, economic and political developments— the spread of white immigrants and the triumph of European civilisation—had specific features which deeply affected the life and fate and fortunes of the Aborigines. As recent historians have insisted, the blacks did not form a coherent or unified 'race', being widely dispersed in space, language, customs and culture. Undisturbed, their shared history would have had its own special rhythms. The reaction of many Aboriginal groupings to the white invasion and spread of settlement led, in a sense, to the very creation of the 'Aborigine', with characteristics and features at least partly imposed by the white settlers, and based as much upon the vicissitudes of human misunderstandings, injustice and historical accident as upon any essential truth or faithful representation of their own aspirations or self-understanding.[11]

The recognition of two quite different experiences of Australia, and perhaps the possibility of their ultimate reconciliation, has been illuminated by the work of the historians. Butlin, for example, describes the dramatically different worlds, societies and expectations of the white and the black inhabitants from the very first aggression. There are of course some over-romantic interpretations of Aboriginal society which exaggerate the achievement, harmony and potential of the first Australians, just as there were hurtful and arrogant underestimates. But, leaving aside the vexed question as to whether some European intervention was or was not inevitable sooner or later (let alone the possibility, in the perspective of a few centuries of history to come, of an eventual Asian 'takeover' of the whole area), the actual settlement of Australia by the British was fraught with prospects of conflict. The coming of the white man, with his cloven-hoofed animals and 'sophisticated' forms of social and economic organisation, overturned the weaker (and hence reputedly more 'primitive') indigenous culture and way of life, and thus created 'winners and losers'.

Land, for example, which was so mystically vital to the original dwellers, and to which the whites became so attached, in sometimes no less real but of course quite different ways, was in the 1830s exploited by the systematic colonisers and others as a resource for sale (so that out of the dividends new migrants might be attracted). Indeed, it takes little exercise of the historical imagination to see that white settlement constituted in many ways a takeover of a relatively successful human enterprise. The Aboriginal economy, now beginning to be understood and appreciated by white scholars, meant a real occupation and tending of the land, and its methods still have much of significance to offer, but it seemed quite outlandish to the settlers at the frontier. It is difficult to see now how an acceptable merger could have taken place between the ancient ways of the Aborigines and the new enterprises of the whalers, sealers, agriculturalists, pastoralists and eventually miners and industrialists of the new dispensation.[12]

The gulfs which existed between the cultures were notable, deep and seemingly irreconcilable at the time. Relations between invaders and original occupants were also tainted by the exercise of power, force and violence, and driven by fear, greed and ethnocentric convictions of superiority. The Aborigines, caught in many toils, reacted from generation to generation in various ways. If there are recognisable themes and patterns which emerge everywhere—of contact, transaction, alienation, confrontation, resistance, collaboration, exploitation, isolation, assimilation, and so on—generalisations are to be avoided as deceptive and essentially de-humanising. Indeed one of the most pervading injustices which has been perpetrated in Australian history lies in the common white misapprehension that what happened was morally blameless—that it was somehow inevitable, following a predestined tragic pathway, and making up peaceful progress of an enlightened pioneering process, in a 'Quiet Continent'.

The history of European colonisation offers many parallel cases, in the southern as well as the northern hemisphere, but almost always there were treaties, and more or less agreed transfers, with compensation and reparations, or else resistance of such proportions that notions of conquest and consequent peacemaking seemed appropriate. The Australian record, now being examined more carefully than ever before, shows neither that the Aborigines surrendered their heritage readily or cravenly nor that they conducted a preternaturally cunning or heroic defence. They fought an often impressive rearguard action—by different means and in different generations—against overwhelming odds and a 'civilisation' which was enabled to enforce its demands, deny compensation to the disinherited, compose and interpret laws to excuse or minimise its theft, and then write its own version of what had happened. Eventually the last insult would be so to marginalise the Aborigines that they became merely part, and a relatively insignificant part at that, of the agenda of a tense, dissatisfied white polity.

Not that all in the Australian experience was unrelievedly bad or vitiated. Ironically, the original aggression was largely unintended and unplanned. It was certainly often unrecognised and only dimly understood. There were many efforts at reconciliation, most of them doomed by failure to recognise the nature and extent of the differences confronted. The lives of blacks and whites included adventures and episodes in co-operation and collaboration as well as litanies of institutionalised prejudice and persistent belittlement. But the confrontation was between two radically different groups, neither understanding the social assumptions or value systems of the other. If Australian history teaches anything, it teaches that understanding and recognition is the only firm foundation for reconciliation.

Even the reconcilers of the past have become subject to re-appraisal. The very notion of 'protectors' was ambiguous. The creation of the office often followed a period of open conflict, and had as one of its objects the maintenance of order. It helped the whites to save face. G.A. Robinson, for example, has been reassessed by Rae Ellis as a 'greedy, vain and unscrupulous man, bent on self-aggrandisement'.[13] Yet the lives and work of humanitarians, high-minded officials and missionaries do show the desire of at least a minority of concerned whites to have direct and conciliatory relations with the blacks. Henry Reynolds, with the balance and scholarship which have earned him universal respect in his field, has provided much fascinating detail as well as a thoughtful analysis of key episodes, figures and movements, and initiated research into the phenomenon of 'collaboration', familiar to students of imperial history elsewhere. In their co-operation with the whites as stockmen, guides and police, the Aborigines in the south-west and south-east of the continent assisted the pioneers: in the north and centre they were the pioneers.

There is no space here to discuss the second onslaught, of missionaries and protectors, as they strove to change and reshape Aboriginal minds and hearts, but work is in progress and at least we have John Harris' virtuoso general history of missionary endeavour, *One Blood*, whose welcome emphasis is on the hopeful and the reconciliatory elements in the story.[14] There were undoubtedly genuine humanitarians, effective battlers and high-minded administrators who stood for justice—heroes and heroines both black and white—as well as meddlers and do-gooders and officious bureaucrats whose ideas, policies and practices led to disasters, scandals and sorrows past all bearing. The whole tale, unvarnished and as authentic and human as can be professionally wrought, is now rapidly becoming more widely known, communicated and reflected upon. The truth can do no harm.

In the effort to discover causes, and to allot blame, the colonising process and the imperial authorities have not escaped attention. James Stephen—the famous Colonial Office official and 'Mr Mothercountry' himself—makes a good enough showing in Reynolds' *Law of the Land*, but is downgraded by A.G.L. Shaw in a recent study. Even Stephen thought nothing short of a miracle would rescue the Aborigines from extermination, though he was tempted at times to teach them 'the art of war and supply them with weapons' to make them formidable and thus to ensure their respectful treatment. He suspected that the policy of reserves would prove to be cruel and confining. Shaw thinks he did not extend to the Aborigines the same humanitarian passion he showed for the negro cause in the West Indies, but left their affairs largely to the politicians.[15]

Yet the attempts to make humane policy stick were real, as Reynolds shows in his careful treatment of the long and involved case of the South Australian Company and its broken promises in the 1840s and 50s. He is very persuasive in arguing that the imperial authorities put more heart into the affairs of the blacks than did the colonial politicians and settlers. In any case, although it was in the nature of the imperial statesmen and officials to seek uniformity of practice (often barely amounting to a recognisable policy), they had to depend ultimately on the man on the spot. Even Stephen usually supported the governors' uses of discretion.

From Phillip on, their instructions urged governors 'to conciliate' the affections of the blacks, 'enjoining all our subjects to live in amity and kindness with them': but such exhortations brought about very mixed results. There also was a sorry history of legal belittlement. The Aborigines were not able to swear oaths in court and hence could give no evidence. Colonial Acts were passed to dispossess the blacks and the Colonial Office, although it examined such laws to see if they were 'repugnant to the laws of England', could not do much, especially after the coming of self-government, although it did try in the cases of South Australia, and, much later in the century, Western Australia. But the colonial politicians were able to write laws and administer policies which increasingly removed the Aborigines as obstacles to white aspirations.[16]

Stephen and others were dealing in their generation with the same basic and perennial questions that returned for consideration in the renewed battle for land rights of the 1970s and after. As Brennan has it, 'Even at the height of the colonial era, there was no doctrine that the colonising sovereign automatically took over unencumbered title to all land in the territory'. This is Reynolds' historical brief in *The Law of the Land*, and he shows that there was always a (minority) view against the reality of *terra nullius* and the other doctrines which were employed to maintain the status quo.

Past injustices can only be addressed, to say nothing of redressed, through a better understanding of the *real* historical facts. The work of historians and others has begun to map the unsound spots in the national memory, and their research and insights have been critical in establishing the causes and outlining the shapes of present ills—and in suggesting possible paths of restitution. It is only by doing painstaking homework that there can be at once a grasp of the extremely complex nature of the social, political, administrative and economic handicaps under which Aborigines have come to live, and any prospect of constructing effective strategies for practical improvement in the future.[17]

The new Australian history shows the contours of present problems in the making (and gives at least hints of feasible solutions). Each era presented fresh dilemmas, e.g. sealing and whaling, the beginnings of agriculture, the growth of the pastoral industry, and the eventual pre-eminence of mining. Traditional Aboriginal ways were devastated by the moving frontier and European methods of enterprise and organisation. It will be important to place in historical memory and context the various landmarks, so as to build on defeats as well as successes. It will also be necessary to recognise and digest the historical style and technique of key Australian institutions, e.g. the three tiers of government, and the consequences of historical fluctuations in the role of the colonial-state governments vis-à-vis the federal commonwealth.

The origins and course of various attempts to isolate, segregate, assimilate, organise, self-help, self-manage, self-determine, and the political history of attempts at reconciliation, (e.g. the 'resolution' of 1988), the proposed 'makarratta' or treaty, and present 'instrument of reconciliation' will have to be taken into consideration, along with the history that went into various platforms and policies of parties, groups and lobbies. The story must be told of the organisation of the Aborigines and Torres Strait Islanders themselves, Federal Council, National Council, and ATSIC. Efforts must be made to place the Australian experience in comparative contexts, e.g. Canada, New Zealand, South Africa, US, so that historical differences and similarities may be discerned and possible precedents uncovered for present tactics and future strategies The role of international law and institutions is relevant and conditioned by history. There is need to know and own our past, to be aware of the facts and clarify the issues.[18]

There have already been excellent regional studies, aimed at reducing that 'cult of forgetfulness' noted by Stanner,[19] and worthy efforts at an overview.[20] But there is need also for more subtle examinations of values and attitudes in time, so as to give an understanding of the belief in the notion of the 'unspoilt savage', and to get behind the theories of ethnocentrism, chauvinism, racial superiority and social Darwinism which proved so potent.[21] If the two cultures are to re-imagine themselves, it is necessary to see what went wrong the first time and afterwards. This journey into the past and into memory must at the same time be a first step into a future of the spirit where visions can be renewed and the dreaming can be refreshed. For the whites, there must be the shock of penitent recognition. As

Pastor Albrecht of the Hermannsburg mission confessed, 'When we first came here we thought we had found the only people in the world without a religion. Now we have learnt that they are among the most religious people in the world'.[22]

Nowadays no general historian would tackle Australian topics without at least an uncomfortable curtsey to the original inhabitants and their special vision. Sir Keith Hancock, noting the end of the earlier 'high optimism' which featured in most historical presentations, had become by 1973 'acutely aware that we owed reparation to the Aborigines' and lamented that 'the gap was conspicuous between our noble professions and our ignoble performance'. The present style is more adamant. W.J. Lines, in his recent *Taming the Great South Land: A History of the Conquest of Nature in Australia*, sums up: 'In under 200 years, a natural world millions of years in the making, and an Aboriginal culture of 60,000 years duration, vanished before the voracious, insatiable demands of a foreign invasion', and writes forthrightly after his examination of the evidence that 'The world's record hardly contains an equivalent to the malicious, unrelenting and unanimous reprobation visited upon the Australian Aborigines. Few national histories contain such odious rationalisation of ugly deeds'. It is all so different from Trollope's grim judgement that 'their doom is to be exterminated; and the sooner their doom be accomplished ... the better will it be for civilisation'.[23]

In the nearest that the Bicentenary produced to an official version, John Mulvaney and Peter White crafted a sensitive reconstruction of Aboriginal society and culture, and Penguin's *A People's History* was fortunate in summoning Henry Reynolds, whose scholarly work has contributed so much to a general revision of both our knowledge and interpretation of the facts, to contribute an excellent piece, 'White Man Came Took Everything'. Russel Ward, doubtless annoyed at the taunt that his influential *The Australian Legend* had 'left the Aborigines out', wrote a whole volume centred on them.[24]

In the ceaseless attempts at defining an Australian identity which Arthur Koestler in 1969 called 'a real problem, and a haunting one' and which now bids fair to becoming a national fashion or obsession, showing few signs of abating as the hunt is taken up by politicians, the 'unfinished business' with the Aborigines is clearly an issue. Manning Clark, in his Boyer Lectures of 1976, laments the 'discourse of the damned' by which white and black in Australia 'could not speak to each other. They were like people on different sides of thick plate glass—only able to see the grief and hatred on each other's faces, but not able to hear, let alone understand what was being said'. Yet he took consolation and gained resolve to help in a process of national reconciliation from the recognition that 'All history is about conflict'.[25]

In short, although the historical reassessment of the Aboriginal role in Australian history has probably been rather the effect than the cause of improvements in the status and expectations of Aborigines, as exemplified by the overwhelming success of the 1967 referendum, the historians clearly have a part to play in redefining and integrating national dreams, in clearing away misconceptions and misjudgements, and in exploring the possibility of an unforced 'cultural convergence'.[26] They will continue to have an important task. The unresolved questions, the half-hidden guilt and anger, the national forgetfulness, and the ambiguities in white attitudes towards the very land itself in space and time, continue to be addressed. The gritty integrity of Aboriginal experience, the depth of individual, family and group strengths exhibited throughout millennia, must receive further analysis. It could provide examples and guides for a future which would, if accompanied by the necessary change of heart and spirit, be based not on polarisation but on positive interaction, peaceful co-existence built on mutual respect, cultural sharing and exchange, dual land ownership and management, and an imaginative emergence of a true 'commonwealth'. This might give the slogans 'one nation' and 'one people' a new truth, meaning and content.

Chapter 2

The Living History of Deaths in Custody

BRIAN McCOY SJ

Some years ago a study was carried out on a farming community in the north-west of America.[1] It found that the farmers there divided up the world inside their heads into three different categories: landscape, machinery and people. Landscape belonged to the trees, the scenery which was not manipulated by the farmers. It was there, something to look at, sometimes to tolerate, sometimes to enjoy. Machinery had a higher value. It was what helped you be productive. Livestock and machines belonged to this category. Machinery was an important and valuable means to an end. People were the third category. They were your neighbours and your friends. They were the people you had grown up with, those you married and those with whom you shared a meal and a drink.

The study showed that not all humans were people. There were the Mexicans, those who helped on the farms and with productivity. They belonged to the machinery class. Their value lay in their contribution to productivity. And there were the Indians. They were looked at and noticed. They belonged to the landscape class. Neither the Mexicans nor the Indians were people. Only some humans were friends, had value in themselves regardless of what they looked like or produced. Only they were seen and treated as people.

This simple study shows how easily we can categorise

and stereotype people whom we perceive as different from ourselves. We can continue to work and live ignoring the deeper reality that we simply do not treat some humans as people. This is what has happened to many of us who live in various Australian cities, towns and communities. We do not see or treat Aborigines as people. It took three years and a $30m Royal Commission to teach us that.

The Royal Commission into Aboriginal Deaths in Custody was a lengthy, costly and wordy affair.[2] The commission reports are extensive in their considerations, especially the *Final Report*'s 339 recommendations. The national commissioner and commissioner for the *Final Report*, Elliott Johnston, continually refers to the men and women who died in custody and from them tries to understand the wider factors and influences which finally lead to the most obvious and compelling conclusion of all: Aborigines die in custody because there are so many in custody.

If other Australians had died at the same rate as Aborigines, over the same period of time of the commission, 7400 would have died, instead of the 400 who did.[3] What the commission quickly discovered was the extremely high rate of Aborigines in custody, in Australia. Aborigines were 27 times more likely to be in police custody, and 11 times more likely to be in prison custody, than other Australians.[4] Commissioner Wootten described such rates as 'quite staggering'.[5] In Western Australia, Aborigines were further over-represented. They were 43 times more likely to be in police custody, and 62 times more likely in prison custody, than non-Aboriginal people.[6] Of the 99 deaths investigated, 32 occurred in Western Australia.

Aborigines account for only 2.69% of the population in Western Australia. Yet, in 1988 they accounted for 54.2% of police custodies and 72% of female police custodies. They accounted for 86.9% of sentenced prisoners serving their sentences in police lockups in 1989 and 51% of sentenced prisoners in prisons during 1988/1989.[7] Of the detentions in police custody, 29% were for public drunkenness and 20% were for 'other good order offences'.[8]

To understand why custody has become a way of life for so many Aborigines, the commission explored each of the various 99 deaths in detail. It also attempted to explore the range of 'underlying issues' which have influenced and continue to influence Aboriginal life.

John Pat's case is a good example of how one death cannot be simply divorced from the history of and issues confronting his Aboriginal community. John Pat's death was one of the major events which triggered the formation of the commission. The manner of his life and death deeply touched many who came to know of his short and tragic life. His death, in the words of the national commissioner, 'became for Aboriginal people nationwide a symbol of injustice and oppression'.[9]

John Pat died in 1983, a month before his seventeenth birthday. He had been arrested outside the Victoria Hotel in Roebourne, after a fight with a number of police officers, all of whom had been drinking and were off duty at the time. It was one particular policeman who, in the opinion of the commissioner, 'bears the main responsibility for the outbreak of the fight'.[10]

After the fight and subsequent arrests the commission found that John Pat and four other prisoners were transferred to the local police station. As they were unloaded from the police vans he and some of the prisoners were then assaulted by the police. At some stage Pat fell to the ground and was then placed unconscious or semi-conscious in a cell. He was found dead later that night, having died of a subdural haemorrhage, a bleeding within the brain. He was also found to have a torn aorta and fractured ribs, both likely to have been sustained around the time of death. While such injuries were consistent with attempts at resuscitation the police officers involved denied that resuscitation had been attempted. He also suffered from internal bleeding around the stomach area.

The commissioner was 'not at all convinced that the evidence of the officers ... [was] true'.[11] Not only were there large gaps in the evidence but there were different accounts by the police and others of the events that night.

The subsequent police investigation was, in the opinion of the commissioner, 'somewhat ineffectual'. Only one of the officers co-operated with the police investigators; the other five involved in the fight and the unloading of the prisoners did not.[12] An inquest into the death resulted in four officers and a police-aide being committed for trial on a charge of manslaughter. Between the inquest and the trial, the coroner wrote to the Attorney-General and outlined various deficiencies in the police investigation. These were referred to the police commissioner who finally 'reported that there was no substance in the coroner's comments'.[13] The police officers were subsequently acquitted by the unanimous verdict of a jury. There was no recommendation by the police that further disciplinary action be taken against the officers.

According to Commissioner Johnston, the verdict of not guilty was the jury's answer to a particular question, namely whether they were satisfied, beyond reasonable doubt, that the five officers, or any one of them, had unlawfully killed John Pat. Unlike the jury, he was able to address other related issues. It was these issues which put John Pat's death into a wider, historical, context.

The commissioner found another side to, another perception of the John Pat the police encountered. Through listening to Aborigines, the commissioner found a young man who was interested in his Aboriginal law and who loved the bush. He liked to draw and to joke. To his mother, he was a son who was happy, never giving her any trouble. When he died, he had been unemployed for almost three years and had been arrested for offences relating to alcohol and assault against police officers. He had never been legally represented on any of the charges and had always pleaded guilty. His first encounter with the police in the lead-up to his death was when he was

walking down the street with three others, carrying an un-
opened bottle of beer. He was charged with two counts of
aggravated assault. John Pat claimed that when he was first
charged, and subsequently charged for further assault offences
against police officers, he had been provoked.

Violence has a long history in the Roebourne area. It
began with the pastoralists who moved into the area in the
1860s and re-shaped and re-named the land.[14] One hundred and
sixteen years before the night of John Pat's death a memorial
was prepared by people at Roebourne 'asking for the "with-
drawal of all Government authority from the district" so that
settlers might work out their own salvation.'[15] As the commissioner pointed out, 'The right of Europeans to take land and to
subjugate, and if necessary eliminate, the rightful owners was
the very foundation of the pastoral industry in the West Pilbara
(as elsewhere). Non-Aboriginal settlers clearly saw their ac-
quisition of land as conquest'.[16] A century later, when equal
pay for Aboriginal workers became law, Aborigines were put
off their traditional lands and ended up in towns like Roebourne.
This development was parallelled by growth of the mining
industry which moved thousands of workers, mainly men, into
the area.[17] This violence to Aborigines, often with a different
face at different times in history, is essentially linked to a
perception of Aborigines as people of lesser value, as less than
people even.

What is particularly illuminating about the John Pat case
is that events from his death up to the commission inquiry are
all determined by non-Aboriginal people. As the commissioner reports, the various incidents surrounding the fight and
the subsequent injury and death were initiated by the police.
The death was followed up by an inadequate inquiry. There
were no Aborigines on the jury. And there was no follow-up to
the trial by the chief superintendent for discipline. In fact 'the
five officers were reinstated to duty on the very day that Mr
Bull reported to the Commissioner'.[18]

What has been described as our 'original sin', that first

perception of Aborigines, often still continues to influence present-day perceptions. These perceptions perpetuate the ways in which newcomers saw the land and justified their taking of it. Aborigines were not allowed to possess their land as Aboriginal nations, as different peoples with their distinctive culture and humanity. There have been 'no less than 67 identifiable classifications, descriptions or definitions' used by governments to describe and determine the nature of Aborigines.[19] An average of a new attempt every three years since 1788!

People were moved from their lands and homes and placed in foreign places. 'Protectors', often the police, were put in control of all aspects of their lives. Children were taken from their parents and placed in homes, boarding schools and other institutions. These were attempts to re-define the distinctive humanity of Aborigines.

The colour of a person's skin became, and in many ways still continues to be, the major criterion by which Aboriginal culture is understood. In 1984 the Federal Government commissioned Australian National Opinion Polls (ANOP) 'to undertake a community attitude research program'[20], to research community attitudes towards Aborigines and related issues. ANOP found that middle Australia saw that there were three groups of Aborigines. There were the '"real" Aboriginal people [who] are tribal, considered to be those full-bloods living a traditional lifestyle'. There were 'educated activists who are almost "white" and totally urbanised'. Then there were the 'half-castes who live in squalor in slums or on the outskirts of towns; [who] spend all their time drinking alcohol, are stranded between two cultures and have little hope for the future'.[21] Perception of a person's colour defined and confined the perception of Aboriginal culture. It then determined what was an expected life style. It predicted behaviour.

This stereotyping of Aborigines, based on physical appearances and colour, was resurrected in the WA Commission when the police union presented its submission. They submitted that there were three groups of Aborigines. Group A were traditional, group B were agricultural and group C were urban (fringe dwellers). 'Traditional' people had a 'pure blood strain', 'agricultural' people were those 'of mixed blood' and 'urban' people were 'the Perth metropolitan and, more recently, Geraldton people, again predominantly of mixed blood and who are referred to as the "fringe dwellers"'.[22] While such a submission, described by the commissioner as 'categorisation … plainly inappropriate and misleading', might represent the current attitudes of police is a concern, that it might represent the broad viewpoint of other Australians is more worrying.

For so long, Aborigines have been perceived in terms of their 'colour' or 'blood line'. The colour test has determined in others' eyes who and what an Aborigine was. It enabled a judgement to be made, without conversation or discussion and much less any understanding of or opinion from the Aboriginal person. Commissioner Wootten explains with an example: 'Colour has always been a basis used by whites to identify who was an Aboriginal person, and the "caste" of children at the Kinchela and Cootamundra Homes was determined by their shading, as happened to David Gundy's cousin when a group of children was taken. At Cootamundra the darkness of the skin determined whether the children were adopted out.'[23]

What non-Aboriginal people saw in terms of colour difference, carefully distinguished from themselves, became the basic criterion for judging any other difference between them and Aborigines. Colour was associated with real cultural differences but these were not examined, appreciated or understood except as belonging to the particular colour of another. Observers confused cultural differences with colour differences and hence generated a world of stereotypes based on a simple perception. This confusion prevented observers from ever understanding Aboriginal cultural differences. Or, as in the case of the police union submission, it provided a superficial and convenient way of judging Aboriginal behaviour.

These attempts to define 'Aboriginality' continue.

Whether it be through the politicians as the law makers, or the police as the law enforcers, the government process is always imposing its views of Aborigines. Such views, in the opinion of the commission, usually stem from a perception of Aborigines as 'the problem', of being 'the white man's burden and in any event his inferior.'[24] The dominant society has worked hard at shaping and defining Aboriginal life on its own terms.

It became obvious to the commissioners that, whatever they might propose or recommend, at the heart of all change some form of reconciliation between non-Aboriginal people and Aborigines was urgently needed. A valuable example of this need for reconciliation was in the extreme responses to the 1989 video of the two police officers who painted their faces black and held nooses around their neck as they mimed the deaths of Lloyd Boney and David Gundy. The airing of the video on national television in March 1992 evoked two very different responses. The president of the NSW Police Association referred to it as 'just a simple attempt at humour'; the Federal Race Relations Commissioner described it as 'symptomatic of deep-seated racism within the police force'.[25] Aborigines do not control the media, education and other attitude-influencing institutions. They are faced with the difficulty of their public definition by other Australians. Stereotyping of Aborigines is often reinforced by the media. Commissioner Dodson commented, 'A form of symbolic apartheid operates with the result that media consumers are presented with an Australia divided into simply "we" and "them" with "we" being normal, stable, rational and peaceful and "them" being abnormal, chaotic, irrational and threatening'.[26] Aborigines have come not only to see themselves negatively portrayed in the media but as 'a race and culture that is different/outside the dominant anglo-celtic realm'.[27] It is not surprising that they, like the compilers of the ANOP survey, despair 'at the extent of the ignorance, intolerance and misunderstanding' in the wider community.[28] Aboriginal poet, Kevin Gilbert, puts it: 'The first casualty in the war of races is the regard for one another's humanity. Whites since colonial days have regarded Aborigines as sub-human and Aborigines, too, doubt the humanity of whites, doubt their capacity for kindness, warmth and natural regard.'[29]

Aborigines had good reason to suspect that their people were being killed in custody. Many factors combined to increase their suspicions, doubts and anxieties concerning the deaths which occurred. The commission did not find any evidence for the hypothesis that there was 'systematic murder or ill-treatment by police officers and prison officers';[30] however it did find that the treatment of Aborigines could and did lead inevitably to a belief by some Aborigines that important information about their relatives' death was being withheld from them. As Commissioner Dodson comments, it is not difficult to presume the worst when one has not been well treated: 'In assessing whether someone is to be trusted, confided in, truthful and honest, it is easy to arrive at an answer if the conduct of the relations under consideration have manifested themselves in a discourteous and inhuman way'.[31] The various reports spoke of the many occasions when information or details about a person's sickness or death was withheld from a family. People were transported to or from custody and their identity was not disclosed. In many cases the family was not advised about where their relative was or, if seriously ill, in what condition. Sometimes people were given incorrect information about a person's illness or place of treatment. As Commissioner Wootten notes in his *Regional Report*, the way people are informed of a death is crucial if families are to believe what they hear or not to become suspicious as to the manner of death.[32] Commissioner Dodson, after listening to Aboriginal people, went further. It was Aborigines, he said, who 'described their relationship with those in authority roles as not satisfactory, racist or inhuman'.[33]

When a person died in custody the subsequent inquiry was often by police officers who were either associated with the circumstances of the death or who were closely connected with officers who had been involved. To Aborigines it was as if relations and family did not have the right to know the circumstances surrounding their relative's death—a right other people in the community would take for granted. Often those associated with a person's death did not appear to care or know how to communicate in a sensitive way what was often shocking and painful news. Aboriginal suspicion that relations had been killed was later increased with coronial inquiries which in many cases were considered by the national commissioner as 'quite perfunctory'.[34]

Families and relations of the deceased had grounds for suspicion because of the low standard of care which Aborigines received in custody. Roy Walker died in the Kalgoorlie lockup in 1981 as a result of a subdural haematoma, a bleeding within the brain. He had been arrested while unconscious and charged with drunkenness. A recommendation was made by the coroner inquiring into his death that persons in the lockup should 'be visited at least hourly, and awoken and spoken to after a reasonable time'.[35] Roy had been visited only once in an eight-hour period. Some years later Faith Barnes was arrested in similar circumstances in the same lockup. Her supervision during the six hours following her custody was inadequate. She also died of a subdural haematoma. The advice of the coroner had not been heeded. With proper care, in the opinion of the national commissioner, her 'death might have been avoided'.[36]

This pattern was repeated in other states. Commissioner Wootten commented on the 'utter indifference' of the Tasmanian police. Not only did they not appear to learn from Glenn Clark's death, and make changes to the circumstances which could assist someone taking their own life, but his own death may have been averted if they had learned from an almost similar death four years previously.[37]

The commission found that on too many occasions Aborigines experienced inadequate care, poor care or even lack of care. Resuscitation equipment was present and available but not used. Aborigines did not receive the quality of care ordinarily due to prisoners, whatever their race or offence. The *National Report* concludes that there was 'in many cases ... the absence of proper care.'[38] Inquiries into the deaths 'disclosed glaring deficiencies in the standard of care afforded many of the deceased during at least portions of their period of incarceration'.[39] At the heart of this indictment was 'what appears ... to have been a lack of commitment to care and a lack of understanding of the importance of care'.[40] When investigations were held into deaths in custody, there was often 'a failure to investigate possible breaches of proper care'.[41] Custodial officers often did not see the importance of treating Aborigines with sensitivity or respect. According to the national commissioner, 'all this reflected a good deal of public apathy in relation to prisoners' conditions'.[42]

The evidence from the cases before the commission suggests that it was more than public apathy which generated this lack of custodial care. Custodial officers did not believe Aboriginal prisoners deserved better care than what they were receiving. Such was the case of Albert Dougal who was found unconscious outside a hotel in Broome, after being assaulted by another person in December 1980. Arresting police assumed he was drunk, despite being informed by the hotel's assistant manager that there had been a fight. Albert could not be roused, smelt strongly of alcohol and was incontinent. Police carried him to their van and took him back to the police station where he was hosed down, left in his wet clothes and then transferred to the concrete exercise yard, without a blanket or mattress, for the night.[43] From 1.00am until 7.30am the station was not staffed. The following morning he was found convulsing and was transferred to the local hospital. The hospital was not told about the fight being the possible cause of unconsciousness. He died of a brain haemorrhage the following day. Commissioner O'Dea concluded: '... by failing to make proper inquiries about the cause of Dougal's unconsciousness, the police deprived him of the chance of early admission to hospital with the result diagnosis was delayed and the prospect of recovery accordingly diminished.'[44]

Commissioner Hal Wootten, in his *Regional Report* states:

> Every one of the deaths was potentially avoidable and in a more enlightened and efficient system of criminal law and justice might not have occurred. Many of those who died should not or need not have been in custody at all, but were there because of archaic laws, unreasonable discretionary decisions for administration of bail, unlawful police actions, or failure to take critically ill people to hospital. Some deaths may have been averted by better custodial practices, more conscientious or more humane attention to prisoners, better psychiatric services in gaol, or proper inquiry into or response to the causes of offences.[45]

The police are seen and used as a powerful arm of the non-Aboriginal community. Whether for the protection of that community, or as a vehicle for controlling the outback, police have undertaken various roles in relation to Aborigines: law enforcer, law interpreter, protector, defender, prosecutor and even punisher. At times, they even took on a military role.[46] In more recent years, Commissioner Wootten points out, they 'have often been perceived as heavily identified with the concerns of the white community, frequently voiced through councils and their committees'.[47] Demands for 'tidy towns' and pleasant urban appearances, set in the age of tourism, have also had their influence on police practices. However, what two different regional reports demonstrate, quite independently, is that in both the east and west of Australia the ratio of police to the population, especially in remote towns with large numbers of Aborigines, is often far in excess of that in the rest of that particular state. In Wilcannia, where Aborigines comprise 80% of the townspeople, there is a police to population ratio of 1:77. In Wiluna, where Aborigines comprise 63%, the ratio is 1:74. The wider police to population state ratio for NSW is 1: 432 and for WA 1:284.[48]

The deaths of Aborigines in custody are not simply related to police numbers and practices. The attitude of police and others in the community to Aborigines has contributed to the deaths. Police differ from the rest of the community by having had a distinctive historical role with Aborigines and by having developed their own identity and even a police culture which Commissioner Wootten explains as 'a set of beliefs, values and attitudes which were wide-spread amongst police officers, highly resistant to change, and passed from one generation of police officers to another.'[49] Part of this police culture is the holding of stereotypes towards groups of people, such as drunks and Aborigines, with the result that it is 'very often difficult to get a policeman to acknowledge the possibility that a person who is intoxicated may also have some other condition which needs attention'.[50] After all, 57% of Aboriginal custodies were for drunkenness.[51]

There is an enormous and a serious gulf between the Aboriginal and non-Aboriginal communities in Australia. It is widened by a perception and treatment of Aborigines by those of the dominant culture which go back to the days when non-Aboriginal people first invaded this land. Feelings of superiority were magnified when the land was declared *terra nullius*. It is very difficult to see someone as a person, much less treat them as one, when the land is claimed to be empty, that people do not exist. The Aborigines, living and hunting in their thousands, constituting some hundreds of separate nations, were viewed as landscape and scenery. They were not dignified with the recognition that they were living on this land, as were other peoples of the world. They were not considered as people worthy of respect, negotiation or a treaty.

The 1967 referendum amended the Commonwealth Constitution to give the commonwealth power to legislate in relation to Aboriginal matters. It was the first attempt to recognise Aborigines. In the words of the *National Report,* this referendum 'demonstrated overwhelming acceptance for the view that Aborigines should be part of the national policy'.[52] For the first time since 1788 they became officially visible.[53] They were to be counted in future census takings and the commonwealth was to legislate for them. This was a far cry from *terra nullius*. However, as Commissioner Dodson comments, such an important change to the lives of Aborigines was once again initiated without any 'negotiations, discussions or decisions over their own affairs and lives'.[54]

It is the need for a new way of seeing Aborigines and culture which lies behind all the inquiries, findings and recommendations of the commission. Australian society must recognise and respect the distinctiveness of Aborigines. Many of the commission's 339 recommendations attempt to extend to Aborigines equality of treatment under the criminal justice system, and also to enhance their own culture and right of self-determination. The last of the 339 recommendations is the most challenging and hardest to implement:

> That all political leaders and their parties recognise that reconciliation between the Aboriginal and non-Aboriginal communities in Australia must be achieved if community division, discord and injustice to Aboriginal people are to be avoided. To this end the Commission recommends that political leaders use their best endeavours to ensure bi-partisan public support for the process of reconciliation and that the urgency and necessity of the process be acknowledged.[55]

The commission hoped that the implementation of its recommendations would 'be carried out in a public way as part of the process of education and reconciliation of the whole society'.[56] We need initiatives to change the fundamental relationship of Aborigines to the major institutions of society, whether they be legal or economic. Before there can be any effective change, the need for such change has to be accepted by the non-Aboriginal community. Often the need is not perceived, much less desired. At the heart of present community division is a limited national recognition that what has occurred is the result of ongoing historical processes determined over 200 hundred years by what non-Aboriginal society first perceived, then created and maintained.

The final paragraph of Commissioner Johnston's *National Report* stresses the hope that a process of reconciliation might bring. He cautions and reminds the non-Aboriginal community: 'I think that patience is required, especially on the non-Aboriginal side. It is the non-Aboriginal society that created the division and sustained it over a long period of time'.[57] He notes that such a process will have its difficulties but will survive 'if we are cool and negotiate with open minds and as equals'.[58] A strong and hopeful vision of equality is the final gift of this very expensive and lengthy commission:

> And in the end, perhaps together, Aboriginal and non-Aboriginal, the situation can be reached where this ancient, subtly creative Aboriginal culture exists in friendship alongside the non-Aboriginal culture. Such an achievement would be a matter of pride not only for all Australians but for all humankind.[59]

Shortly after the *National Report* and regional reports were published there was much hesitation by state and federal governments in responding to the commission's findings and recommendations. In Western Australia the Premier announced on Friday 10 May 1991, the day when the reports were first made available to the public, that her state government would 'establish a special task force to investigate whether further prosecutions or disciplinary action should be taken against police and prison officers over Aboriginal deaths in custody'.[60] In the next few days, the premier discovered that she did not have the support she had presumed. Three days later the headline ran: 'Cabinet split over black deaths probe'.[61] The following day the paper announced: 'Premier reneges on tough probe stand'.[62] Her plans for a task force were scrapped. This about-face by the government did little to generate confidence in the community that the government was committed to facing and changing the difficult and unpleasant truths about its treatment of Aborigines. Nor was any further confidence generated when Police Minister Graham Edwards announced that disciplinary action was unlikely in the John Pat case because of the time since the event.[63]

Like those farmers in the north-west of America, we Australians can come to see our way of life as a given, something we accept as unchangeable. The farmers did not realise that they did not treat different cultural groups as people. The content within people's minds and hearts determines how they perceive and treat others. However, we do have the ability to change our stereotypes and perceptions. New legislation will make some difference. The young and the educated are ones who are particularly open to change. But the beginning of any lasting and effective change is a recognition that all is not as it is should be. Prime Minister, Paul Keating has said, 'Until we start to make some real progress towards closing the gap in both attitudes and living standards, I think there will always be that feeling among us that maybe we don't quite belong, that we're not quite serious, that we're simply here for the view.'[64] It will be a tragedy if we continue to live with the same view we have had for the past 205 years.

Chapter 3

From *Terra Nullius* to Constitutional Recognition of Aboriginal Rights

FRANK BRENNAN SJ

The Barunga Statement

While government ministers speak of reconciliation, Aboriginal leaders speak of treaties, self-determination, land rights and sovereignty. While the High Court of Australia has exploded the myth that the country was *terra nullius* at the time of colonisation, the Australian parliament has set up a Council for Aboriginal Reconciliation to promote a process of reconciliation between Aborigines and Torres Strait Islanders and the wider Australian community. It is a far cry from the treaty process proposed by Prime Minister Hawke when he met with Aboriginal leaders at the Barunga Sports and Cultural Festival during the Bicentenary. Courtesy of Bob Hawke in the dying minutes of his prime ministership, the Barunga statement, which is a land council sponsored charter of Aboriginal rights from the Northern Territory, now hangs in Parliament House, Canberra. It will hang as a constant reminder that indigenous rights are about more than alleviating poverty, combating disadvantage, and rectifying dispossession.

As parties to the statement, the Northern and Central Land Councils spoke for 'the Indigenous owners and occupiers of Australia' in their call on the Australian government and people to recognise their rights:

• to self-determination and self-management, including the freedom to pursue our own economic, social, religious and cultural development;
• to permanent control and enjoyment of our ancestral lands;
• to compensation for the loss of our lands, there having been no extinction of original title;
• to protection of and control of access to our sacred sites, sacred objects, artefacts, designs, knowledge and works of art;
• to the return of the remains of our ancestors for burial in accordance with our traditions;
• to respect for and promotion of our Aboriginal identity, including the cultural, linguistic, religious and historical aspects, and including the right to be educated in our own languages and in our own culture and history;
• in accordance with the Universal Declaration of Human Rights, the International Covenant on Economic, Social and Cultural Rights, the International Covenant on Civil and Political Rights, and the International Convention on the Elimination of All Forms of Racial Discrimination, rights to life, liberty, security of person, food, clothing, housing, medical care, education and employment opportunities, necessary social services and other basic rights.

They called on the commonwealth to pass laws providing:

• a national elected Aboriginal and Islander organisation to oversee Aboriginal and Islander affairs;
• a national system of land rights;
• a police and justice system which recognises our customary laws and frees us from discrimination and any activity which may threaten our identity or security, interfere with our freedom of expression or association, or otherwise prevent our full enjoyment and exercise of universally recognised human rights and fundamental freedoms.

They asked that the Australian government support Aborigines in the development of an international declaration of principles of indigenous rights, leading to an international covenant, and called on the commonwealth parliament 'to negotiate with us a treaty recognising our prior ownership, continued occupation and sovereignty and affirming our human rights and freedoms.'

At the time the statement was presented to Hawke, he and his Minister for Aboriginal Affairs, Gerry Hand, signed an agreement with land council representatives Galarrwuy Yunupingu and Wenten Rubuntja:

1. The government affirms that it is committed to work for a negotiated treaty with Aboriginal people.
2. The government sees the next step as Aborigines deciding what they believe should be in the treaty.
3. The government will provide the necessary support for Aboriginal people to carry out their own consultations and negotiations: this could include the formation of a committee of seven senior Aborigines to oversee the process and to call an Australia-wide meeting or convention.
4. When Aborigines present their proposals the government stands ready to negotiate about them.
5. The government hopes that these negotiations can commence before the end of 1988 and will lead to an agreed treaty in the life of this Parliament.

No treaty did result before Mr Hawke left office. However, after his last election, Mr Hawke did write to Dr Hewson, leader of the opposition, advising him 'of the Government's wish to achieve a more bipartisan approach in furthering the welfare of the Aborigines and Torres Strait Islanders and advancing the concept of an instrument of reconciliation'.[1] The Prime Minister said, 'It is our intent to continue to consult with the Coalition and seek a bipartisan approach on these matters. There will also be a need for early consultations with the states, church leaders and others.' Opening the new parliament in May 1990, the Governor-General Mr William Hayden announced:

[The Government] will be seeking wide community support and bipartisan political endorsement of an instrument of reconciliation, variously referred to as a Treaty or Compact, between Aboriginal and Torres Strait Islander Australians and the wider Australian community.

The form and content of such a document will not and cannot be finalised until extensive consultation is initiated with Aboriginal and Torres Strait Islander people and other Australians. This process of consultation will be enhanced following the recent establishment of the Aboriginal and Torres Strait Islander Commission.

After intense discussion in the shadow cabinet, Dr Hewson replied, treating Hawke's letter as a 'sounding out' of the coalition's support for a process of reconciliation:

I would point out, as stated specifically in our current policy, that the Coalition 'is open to consideration of proposals which will improve relationships between Aborigines and other Australians'. It is not possible, however, to give any firm commitment to a more bipartisan approach to a process of reconciliation at this stage until we know precisely what it is you intend to propose.

You acknowledge that the Coalition recognises the importance of reconciliation and, to this end, we would like to know how you intend to proceed with regards to a process of reconciliation as there may be room for considerable common ground.[2]

Mr Hawke had paid tribute to the coalition's achievements when in government for the betterment of Aborigines through measures that 'received strong bipartisan support'. Pleading for a return to bipartisanship, he claimed broad agreement between the parties on some objectives including Aboriginal self-sufficiency and improvements in health, education, employment and housing. Dr Hewson welcomed the call to bipartisanship as a significant break with the recent past. He claimed that the bipartisan approach had been broken by the Labor government's 'pursuit of the National Land Rights legislation, your Treaty proposal and ATSIC' (the Aboriginal and Torres Strait Islander Commission set up to replace the Aboriginal Development Commission and the Department of

Aboriginal Affairs). Critical of insufficiently monitored programs, duplication of services and administrative inefficiencies, Dr Hewson was sure that Mr Hawke would understand 'that we would not want a more bipartisan approach to limit us from criticising your Government so long as we perceive these issues as being inadequately addressed.'

Seeking to avoid the semantic debate about the word 'treaty', Mr Hawke had said he was not wedded to the term. He was open to other terms for 'a form of instrument of reconciliation':

> What I believe is important is that there be a process of reconciliation. In my view, the consultation processes will be as important as the eventual outcome. But there is little hope of a worthwhile outcome, even to consultations, without the support of the majority of Australians.
>
> I understand that in the recent past the Coalition, on the basis of an assumption that the nature of a 'treaty' involves an agreement between two nations, has stated its opposition to such a cause. I assure you that it has never been in the Government's mind that the reconciliation process lead to such an outcome.

Despite the reservations of some Aboriginal leaders, the instrument, whatever it might be called, was to have no implications whatever in international law. Dr Hewson restated the coalition's objections to a treaty or anything like it by another name:

> Our opposition to a treaty is based on our strongly held belief that Australians belong to one nation and one group of Australians cannot have a treaty with the rest of the nation.
>
> It has been our consistent position since 1981 that a treaty has implications in international law which are unacceptable to the Australian people.

Whatever the Liberal and National Parties have been opposing, it is not what the Labor Party was ever proposing in government. Back in 1981 when in government, the coalition parties were prepared to contemplate a negotiated agreement with Aborigines subject to constraints and having no effect in international law.

The coalition has long been critical of the Labor government since 1983 having resort to 'highly symbolic gestures in place of a careful and continuing attention to the administration of effective programmes'. This false dichotomy between the symbolic and the material overlooks the possibility that there is a need for effective programmes as well as symbolic gestures. Without effective programmes, symbolic gestures will be a sham anyway. Dr Hewson still maintains a suggestion of the dichotomy:

> In our view, an ongoing process of reconciliation and adequate positive programs and material support which leads to a significant improvement in the standard of living, quality of life and self esteem of Aboriginal Australians would enhance their cause in a more meaningful way than a treaty or similar instrument.

When Patrick Dodson concluded his role as commissioner on the Royal Commission into Aboriginal Deaths in Custody, he spoke of the need for land and better services for Aboriginal communities being a necessary part of the process of reconciliation and a pre-condition for any instrument of reconciliation. For him, 'to reconcile people is a noble thing to do, but it is also a practical and essential thing to do, if we are going to reduce the levels of expenditure that we currently have for police, health and special types of programmes to tackle the backlog of needs that exist in Aboriginal communities.'[3]

The Council for Aboriginal Reconciliation

The Hawke-Hewson correspondence set down the narrow confines within which the parliament was prepared to give its unanimous endorsement to the Council for Aboriginal Reconciliation which was established in September 1991 and met for the first time in February 1992. There is no reason why there should not be both a process and an instrument of reconciliation.

Reconciliation can be effected by the exercise of collective responsibility for our present social reality; it will not be furthered by harping on collective guilt for the past. In this our national politicians could have a role to play. There are three separate questions to be answered in the process.

First, what do Aborigines want? There is a wide variety of Aboriginal viewpoints. Some, like Michael Mansell, will not be party to any process which presumes them to be Australian citizens. They claim to be Australian Aborigines rather than Aboriginal Australians subject to the laws and policies of Australian governments. They assert a sovereignty which has never been voluntarily surrendered. They see domestic treaty talk as a denial of their separate nation status. Like anyone else, they are entitled to their viewpoint, though they might not be right and it might not get them anywhere. Others like Charles Perkins proudly see themselves as part of the Australian nation. Perkins has said, 'Aboriginal people would do well to consider that, in the coming decade, they can gain benefits for themselves and the nation by playing a more involved role in areas beyond Aboriginal affairs.'[4] If the Mansell viewpoint enjoyed wide support among Aborigines, there would be no point in the government proceeding with any process of reconciliation premissed on Aborigines being citizens seeking recognition, rights and reconciliation under Australian law and through the Australian government. If the Perkins view was shown to reflect the aspirations of most Aborigines, there would be point in proceeding.

Second, what are the moral entitlements of Aborigines? What additional rights ought Aborigines have under Australian law, not just because they are poor, disadvantaged or dispossessed but because they are *Aboriginal*, the descendants of the traditional owners of this land and the primary custodians of the culture which is unique to this society? Such entitlements are unlikely to take the form of individual rights en-

forceable in the courts. But there may be collective entitlements capable of respect and recognition by governments and
other citizens. In this, Aborigines are not the only experts in
justice and morals. For example, many, including non-Aborigines, would concede that Aborigines in some circumstances
do have a moral claim to land which is their traditional country.

Third, what is politically achievable? Messrs Keating,
Hewson and their minders may be better informed in answer-
ing this question than Messrs Perkins, Mansell and theirs.
Australians generally have no absorbing concern about an
agreement between two separate parties distinguished on the
basis of race two centuries after the first wave of non-Aboriginal migration. But they may be open to negotiating and guar-
anteeing the place of Aborigines in the commonwealth, while
reviewing and overhauling the Constitution in the lead-up to
its first centenary. There is no reason why a mature nation
should deny itself the opportunity of using its Constitution to
express the fundamentals of its identity as a nation state.

Sovereignty, land rights and *terra nullius*

It is ten years since five Torres Strait Islanders commenced
proceedings in the High Court of Australia claiming traditional
land title over their islands. By the time the case was decided,
only two of them were still living. But, thanks to their efforts,
the myth of *terra nullius* has been exploded by an overwhelming majority of six to one in the High Court. This was the first
time our highest court considered the legal arguments about
sovereignty and land rights. Land rights are here to stay—not
as special welfare measures, but as equal protection of all
citizens under the law. The Rev. David Passi and Mr James
Rice, together with the late Mr Eddie Mabo (under whose
name the case is identified) and two others now deceased,
commenced proceedings as the representatives of the traditional owners of three islands in the Murray Islands group.

They claimed that the islands had been continuously

inhabited and exclusively possessed by their people who lived in permanent settled communities with their own social and political organisation. They claimed that the annexation of their islands by the governor and parliament of Queensland in 1879, though extending sovereignty of Queen Victoria to the islands, did so subject to the continued enjoyment of their rights until those rights had been extinguished by the sovereign. Further they claimed that their rights had not been validly extinguished and that their continued rights were recognised by the Australian legal system.

The Queensland government's lawyers thought the Islanders might have a case. They were right. Sir Joh Bjelke-Petersen took a gamble and attempted to short circuit the legal proceedings. In 1985 the Queensland parliament passed the Queensland Coast Islands Declaratory Act innocuously described as an Act 'to allay doubts that may exist concerning certain islands forming part of Queensland'. The Act declared that, upon the islands being annexed in 1879, they were 'vested in the Crown in right of Queensland freed from all other rights, interests and claims of any kind whatsoever'. It provided that no compensation would be paid for rights retrospectively taken away.

Introducing the legislation, Mr William Gunn, the then Deputy Premier, said: 'The passage of this Bill will, it is hoped, remove the necessity for limitless research work being undertaken in relation to the position of the relevant Torres Strait Islands prior to annexation and will prevent interminable argument in the courts on matters of history'.[5] The legislation failed to achieve its purpose. It resulted in two High Court cases rather than one.

In the first case, in 1988, the Queensland Coast Islands Declaratory Act was challenged by the Murray Islanders. The High Court ruled that the Queensland legislation was contrary to the Racial Discrimination Act which had been enacted by the commonwealth parliament to implement the International Convention on the Elimination of all Forms of Discrimination.

Three judges of the High Court described the 'draconian' effect of the Queensland law 'to extinguish the rights which the plaintiffs claim in their traditional homeland and to deny the right to compensation in respect of that extinction'.

In the second case, the High Court heard argument that the Torres Strait Islanders retained property rights after the Crown asserted sovereignty over their islands. The commonwealth government withdrew from the proceedings at the earliest opportunity—seeing land rights as a state matter and having no desire to advocate such rights in the nation's highest court. Given this was the first opportunity for the High Court to consider the basis of Aboriginal land tenure in this country, it is extraordinary that the commonwealth had nothing to say.

For the first time, the High Court has set down the law of the land on just foundations which will provide a new basis for negotiating a fair sharing of the country at those new frontiers where miners, pastoralists and governments will meet Aboriginal landholders as if for the first time. The court has ruled that 'the common law of this country recognises a form of native title which, in the cases where it has not been extinguished, reflects the entitlement of the indigenous inhabitants, in accordance with their laws and customs, to their traditional lands'. The Torres Strait Islanders in the case are entitled 'as against the whole world to possession, occupation, use and enjoyment' of their lands. Though the governor and parliament of Queensland retain the sovereign power to extinguish the title, they cannot do so unless they comply with all relevant laws including the Commonwealth's Racial Discrimination Act. So the holders of native title are guaranteed the same protection from government interference and expropriation as any other titleholders to land.

Where Aborigines and Islanders still have traditional relationships with their land and where that land is not subject to a freehold grant or lease to others and where it is not being used for a public purpose inconsistent with the continuation of native title, those indigenous Australians retain a special title to their land in accordance with their own law and customs. That title is recognised by the courts of Australia. Aborigines may have a legal claim to interest in national parks throughout Australia. They may have native title over vacant Crown land even if a mining company is prospecting, exploring or mining under the land. They may have title to stock routes. They could even have title to lands subject to grazing licences. In each case it is a question of whether the native title has been extinguished and that depends on whether 'the Crown has validly alienated land by granting an interest that is wholly or partially inconsistent with a continuing right to enjoy native title'.

Justice Brennan (with Chief Justice Mason and Justice McHugh agreeing) has said: 'Where the Crown has not granted interests in land or reserved and dedicated land inconsistently with the right to continued enjoyment of native title by the indigenous inhabitants, native title survives and is legally enforceable'. Having said it was conceivable that the whole of the Australian continent was affected previously by common law native title, Justices Deane and Gaudron said: 'The power of the Crown wrongfully to extinguish the native title by inconsistent grant will remain but any liability of the Crown to pay compensatory damages for such wrongful extinguishment will be unaffected'.

Exploding the myth of *terra nullius*, Justice Brennan said: 'The fiction by which the rights and interests of indigenous inhabitants in land were treated as non-existent was justified by a policy which has no place in the contemporary laws of this country.' He went on to say, 'The common law of this country would perpetuate injustice if it were to continue to embrace the enlarged notion of *terra nullius* and to persist in characterising the indigenous inhabitants of the Australian colonies as people too low in the scale of social organisation to be acknowledged as possessing rights and interests in land'.

Justices Deane and Gaudron admitted the need for 'unusually emotive' language in their judgment, speaking of the oppression and near obliteration of Aborigines as 'the inevitable consequences of their being dispossessed of their traditional lands'. They said, 'The lands of this continent were not *terra nullius* or practically unoccupied in 1788. The Crown's property in the lands of the Colony of New South Wales was ... reduced or qualified by the burden of the common law native title of the Aboriginal tribes and clans to the particular areas of land on which they lived or which they used for traditional purposes.'

When Eddie Mabo and his fellow Islanders commenced their litigation ten years ago, Sir Joh Bjelke-Petersen had been telling us of 'a Communist long-range plan to alienate Aboriginal lands from the Australian nation so that a fragmented north could be used for subversive activities by other countries'.[6] Those days are well behind us. Perhaps we are coming to terms with the justice demanded by our history. In another ten years we should even be able to acknowledge this history and its just demands in our Constitution. There can be no reconciliation without due recognition and equal protection of everyone's property rights under the law.

Self-determination

Since 1982, many indigenous groups have been pressing the UN Working Group on Indigenous Populations (WGIP) to recognise their entitlement to self-determination within the legal framework of the nation states built on their dispossession without consent or compensation.

Within Australia, the most appropriate forum for consideration of the limits of self-determination will be the Council for Aboriginal Reconciliation which has a statutorily guaranteed life until 1 January 2001. The ten-year-old word games about treaties and sovereignty have meant the council's establishment has been clouded in suspicion. There has never been any prospect of the commonwealth, state and territory governments negotiating an agreement conceding or ceding sovereignty to an Aboriginal nation or nations.

There is no prior legal or philosophical reason why areas

such as Torres Strait and Arnhem Land could not be constituted as states of the federation or even as separate nations
some time in the future. The usual provisos of discrete territory, people and economic base, together with consent of
affected persons, may be able to be met in the distant future,
especially if there were to be major oil discoveries in the
Torres Strait. A compact of free association with mainland
Australia could deal with defence and foreign policy issues.
But there is no indication of overwhelming desire for such a
regime from the traditional residents of these areas. They are a
long way from economic and service self-sufficiency. They
find advantages as well as disadvantages in being part of the
Australian nation. Many see themselves as and want to remain
Australians, albeit recognised and respected as the indigenous
peoples of the continent.

Even if Aborigines in Redfern, Fitzroy or West End
wanted separate statehood within the federation, or nationhood, they would be ineligible as they lack a discrete land base
with readily identifiable boundaries. Their yearnings for self-
determination would have to be realised within the states and
territories of the federation composed of a mix of races. For
them, constitutional and legal accommodation within the Australian nation is the only way to go. This does not necessarily
entail assimilation or integration. Within the constitutional
framework, they could be accorded greater autonomy as discrete communities for the governance of matters relating only
to members of those communities. The difficulty in setting
limits would arise between the rights of an individual who
wants to be treated like any other Australian (e.g. not being
forced into a traditional marriage or initiation process) and the
entitlement of the community to order its affairs according to
customary law so as to maintain and preserve the culture.
There would have to be guaranteed opting out procedures.

In the political process, we are yet to move beyond the
paternalistic phase of open-ended consultation to negotiation
within agreed or non-negotiable parameters. Romantic rheto-

ric about some monolithic and mythical Aboriginal nation and unyielding insistence that all Australians be treated the same, as if there were no indigenous peoples with rights and entitlements before 1788 whose descendants ought continue to enjoy recognition as custodians of culture as well as legal protection from further dispossession without consent, have to give way to a creative partnership in exploring the possibilities for maximum indigenisation within the life of the nation subject to inevitable economic and social constraints.

At the very least, Aborigines ought be able to call the executive arm of government to account before an independent tribunal for practices or policies inconsistent with the entitlement to self-determination. Our legislatures should be required by the Constitution to legislate subject to Aboriginal law in circumstances where all parties are Aborigines who consent to Aboriginal law prevailing. Our courts should apply Aboriginal law when all parties including a victim's closest kin are Aboriginal and agree to such law applying. Aboriginal law would be best set down by Aboriginal councils and applied by Aboriginal courts. Even these limited incidences of self-determination within a more diverse nation may not be sought by most Aborigines. As a nation we need to hear the aspirations of contemporary indigenous Australians and then debate their moral entitlements.

At the end of the sit-in by Aborigines in the old Parliament House on Australia Day 1992, the National Aboriginal and Islander Legal Services Secretariat (NAILSS) acting 'on behalf of the Aboriginal nation' presented the Minister for Aboriginal Affairs, Mr Robert Tickner, with a declaration of Aboriginal sovereignty:

> We, the members of the Aboriginal Nation and Peoples, do hereby give notice of invoking our claim to all the land of the Territories of our ancestors. Accordingly, we invoke the Rule of International Law that we have never surrendered nor acquiesced in our claim to these lands and territories. This occupation of the site of the old

Parliament building is evidence of our right to self-government and self-determination in our lands and territories.

We therefore draw the attention of the International Community and the United Nations to our peaceful and lawful right of occupation of our lands and territories.

It is for Aboriginal leaders to determine their political strategy of ambit claims and rhetoric which effects a shift in the goal posts or middle ground. However, inflated rhetoric from a minority always risks further alienation from the majority, especially if the self-interest of the majority is threatened even if only in the fertile imaginations of the minority's greatest critics.

Self-determination subject to the constitution and laws of the Commonwealth of Australia ought now be seen as a non-controversial statement of the legitimate and recognizable aspirations of Aborigines seeking maximum community independence while remaining part of the nation state.

The way ahead: reconciliation through just recognition

Aborigines will gain little by abandoning the word games of Canberra in favour of the word games of Geneva. If they contribute to the debate in both fora within the predetermined and immovable parameters, they may gain more room to move on their lands, permitting the transformation of land rights from a simple issue of land title to one of community self-determination. This will require use of the Council for Aboriginal Reconciliation back home as well as the WGIP in Geneva. All major political parties should now acknowledge the right of self-determination in the domestic sense. An accurate delimitation of the scope of self-determination by Aboriginal advocates will be more productive than the expansive rhetoric of sovereignty, unless the politics of ambit claims is still judged more efficacious than the negotiation of achievable and justifiable rights.

As chairperson of the Council for Aboriginal Reconciliation, Patrick Dodson now has the difficult task of convincing Aboriginal groups to back the council which has a decade to investigate the desirability of an 'instrument of reconciliation'. He is right when he claims: 'The question that must be directed to critics of the process is what is the practical alternative to reconciliation? I think the only alternative is to do nothing. I believe we have reached a stage in our evolution as a nation where neither Aboriginal nor non-Aboriginal Australians can afford for that to happen.'[7] Trouble is, there will be some Aboriginal groups who think they will be better off with nothing. Some Aborigines are so mistrustful of Australian political processes that they see no gain in negotiating concessions within parameters set by non-Aboriginal moral argumentation and domestic political realism. They see no point in getting things settled so the line can be drawn. They would prefer sporadic gains and the assurance after each encounter that the last word has not been spoken on Aboriginal rights. For them, treaty talk is the invention of moralising, bourgeois non-Aborigines anxious to solve their own problems and to clean up the nation's backyard before the international spotlight zeros in. Some Aborigines see future international embarrassment without a treaty as their chief political lever.

In 1987, 58% of Australians polled supported the idea of a treaty. The latest poll shows 65%. Young people, alive to the music of Yothu Yindi and emerging as the first school graduates to have undertaken Aboriginal studies in their curriculum, are 83% in favour of a treaty.[8] Naturally the percentages in rural areas are less. Even those in favour have little sense of what the process or content of any treaty would be. If constitutional recognition of indigenous rights is to be on the agenda, majority approval will be essential. Aboriginal rights will have to piggyback on more mainstream issues such as the republic and a bill of rights. No Aboriginal measure will progress unless it has the support of all major political parties. Dodson and his followers are right when they say there is no alternative to the Council for Aboriginal Reconciliation if constitutional entrenchment of rights is to be even theoretically under consideration, let alone actually placed on the political agenda. On Columbus Day, 12 October 1992, we marked the 500th anniversary of his discovery of the Americas. Indigenous peoples reminded us that Columbus discovered nothing which had not already been discovered, inhabited, and reflected upon for centuries by entire societies which were to suffer the down-side of colonisation—dispossession, subjugation and even death. That day, the UN Secretary General formally opened the International Year for the World's Indigenous Peoples with the theme 'Indigenous Peoples—A New Partnership'. The Australian government in welcoming the UN initiative said, 'It will be an opportunity to reflect further on what the right to self-determination means for indigenous peoples.'⁹

Robert Tickner, Minister for Aboriginal Affairs in the Keating government, has taken his lead from the Royal Commission into Aboriginal Deaths in Custody and enunciated self-determination as a key concept of government policy. The Department of Foreign Affairs and Trade has recently suggested that with changes in the international system, 'the concept of self-determination must be considered broadly, as peoples seek to assert their identities to preserve their languages, cultures and traditions and to achieve greater autonomy, free from undue interference by central governments. The challenge to governments is to respond effectively to the growing demands of indigenous peoples in this area.'¹⁰ Self-determination subject to the constitution and laws of the Commonwealth of Australia ought now be seen as a non-controversial statement of the legitimate and recognizable aspirations of Aborigines seeking maximum community independence while remaining part of the nation state.

In the decade ahead, those Aborigines opposed to a treaty negotiation process aimed at entrenching domestic self-determination for Aboriginal and Islander communities and groups will be joined by miners and pastoralists motivated by their own self-interest. Those Aborigines seeking incremental gains at home will add local self-determination to land rights, local community government and Aboriginal participation in the administration of government service programmes thus maximising their hopes of doing their own thing and maintaining their culture within the Australian nation. They will face many obstacles. They will not get there alone. But they have some strong allies including the recently formed Constitutional Centenary Foundation chaired by Sir Ninian Stephen. The High Court's decision in the *Mabo* case has now discredited the *terra nullius* doctrine and opened the gates for a new understanding of land rights and self-management proposals. Addressing land rights and self-determination, we are not concerned with welfare measures but with the recognition of property and personal rights under the rule of law.

Approaching the first centenary of our existence as a federation under the Constitution, we have the time to negotiate a just and proper settlement. It is time to share this country on just terms even with its traditional owners. Committed to finding common ground, we need to ensure that no Australian be alien to the land or to the society which is our common heritage. Overcoming the differences caused by poverty, disadvantage and dispossession, and respecting the differences between indigenous and other cultures and lifestyles, we can be reconciled as a nation and as people, owning our past and shaping our future, according justice and recognition to all. We might then share the country with all belonging to this land.

Chapter 4

Aboriginal Self-determination

WILLIAM DANIEL SJ

With the fifth centenary of the 'discovery' of the Americas by Columbus upon us, and the International Year of Indigenous Peoples in the offing, considerable attention is being paid to the situation of indigenous peoples and to ways in which some of the devastation of the colonial period might be undone, and some of the rights of the subject peoples restored.

The rights that the indigenous peoples worldwide are pursuing are those set forth in the United Nations International Covenants on Economic, Social and Cultural Rights and on Civil and Political Rights:

> All peoples have the right of self-determination. By virtue of that right they freely determine their status and freely pursue their economic, social and cultural development.[1]

The peoples here envisaged are the peoples who occupied the territories vacated by colonial powers in the decolonisation process, and who formed national governments, whether on natural boundaries, or within the artificial and sometimes arbitrary divisions drawn up by the colonial powers.

This right to self-determination is freely acknowledged when it is claimed by new nations lately decolonised. It is another matter when similar rights are claimed by indigenous peoples within the framework of a nation state. This is the agenda which is shaping up in the Americas, and in Australia and New Zealand. India and China insist that there are no indigenous peoples within their territories, only minorities. The semantics involved here do not conceal the fact that there are within the borders of these and many other nations ethnic groups which regard themselves as strangers in their own country and as victims of an alien oppression. The nation state as we know it is not one of the eternal facts of political life, and we may well be living in its dying phases. The break-up of the Soviet empire and the fragmentation taking place in the Balkans may be the beginning of a process whose outcome cannot at this stage be foreseen. The push for recognition and autonomy by various ethnic minorities worldwide seems to be stimulated by the power that is placed in their hands by modern communications, even as the same technology is being used by governments in an attempt to keep them sedated or under control.

The United Nations Working Group on Indigenous Populations (WGIP), meeting in August 1991, published a draft Declaration on Indigenous Rights, which includes a working definition of the right to self-determination:

> Indigenous people have the right to self-determination. By virtue of this right, they freely determine their relationship with the states in which they live, in a spirit of co-existence with other citizens, and freely pursue their economic, social, cultural and spiritual development in conditions of freedom and dignity.[2]

I propose to take this as a working definition of self-determination.

Which peoples are indigenous?

The Celtic peoples of Wales and Cornwall are indigenous with respect to the Anglo-Saxon hordes who came after them. Could they claim the right to self-determination as outlined in the WGIP Declaration? Does the passage of time extinguish such rights? Does acquiescence in the status quo over many centuries? The drive for Scottish national independence *need* not be seen as a matter of rights, but rather as a matter of political preference; and a British government which acceded to this demand *need* not be seen to be granting the Scots their rights, but rather bowing to the politically inevitable.

Fortunately the case with which we are concerned, namely the Aboriginal people of Australia, is not one which must be traced back into the mist of centuries. The occupation of their land by European invaders took place in the recent past and it is well documented. And there is no sense in which the Europeans and the Aborigines have come to form one population, as might be said of the diverse inhabitants of Great Britain over the centuries.

Indigenous peoples or minorities?

The concept of self-determination is often viewed with alarm by those who see it as a formula for the disintegration of our society. If the Aborigines are allowed self-determination, they argue, the next to want it will be the Italians, followed by the Turks and the Vietnamese.

The special claim made for indigenous peoples is not based on the fact that they are different, but that the land was theirs and was taken from them, and that they had a culture and it was overwhelmed by the invading culture. And all this was done in most cases without reference to their wishes or rights. Latter-day migrants, on the other hand, however different they may be from the majority of the population, have come to Australia of their own free will (disregarding the case of our convict forebears) seeking a place in Australian society for their own purposes. It is good that ethnic diversity be recognised, and the riches of different cultures be preserved, but the voluntary migrant has a simple duty to fit into the social structure and order of his or her adopted country.

Indigenous people or persons?

Certain philosophers have scruples about awarding rights or responsibilities to groups, on the grounds that rights should be predicated only of individual persons.[3] This surely is individualism carried to an extreme. If there is such a thing as a right of association, e.g. in trade unions or religious bodies, this right would surely be nugatory if those same associations could not be accorded civil rights and obligations. With regard to the Australian Aborigines, the problem of group as opposed to individuals is the problem of identifying the group, and of finding people to speak for it. No doubt there is a common heritage of aboriginality in all the groups, but it is an oversimplification to think of them as one people when they differ so much from one part of Australia to another, from city to country, from the more settled to those living the traditional tribal life. To speak of self-determination for such a diverse group of people is to face a situation of great complexity, and one which is not going to be resolved by the simple application of some European or western political formula.

Wants and needs and rights

The language of human rights has suffered from overuse in recent years. It has been high season for the ancient dictum of the logicians: *Quod gratis asseritur, gratis negatur*—what is asserted without proof can be denied without proof. To quote David Hollenbach:

> The simple fact that someone makes a claim does not mean that the claim must be respected … People sometimes make impossible, illegal, even immoral claims and occasionally they use the language of rights when they do so. The determination of which claims are justified and therefore qualify as human rights is a crucial task.[4]

As Hollenbach shows very well in his *Claims in Conflict*,[5] Christian theory of rights is based on the doctrine of the creation of human beings in the image and likeness of God. Created and redeemed, they are destined for life with God, and are endowed with a corresponding dignity. The being thus endowed has certain needs if the being is to flourish and that dignity is to be respected.

These needs will provide the basis for various necessary liberties and claims. If dignity is to be preserved, the human being needs freedom from physical injury, freedom to associate, freedom of belief and worship, freedom to marry and found a family. If the person is to survive and flourish, various claims must be met by society at large—for example, the need for food and shelter, for education, for work, for participation in the political process.

These latter claims are conditional upon the ability of a society to meet them. The claim for food and health care cannot be met at a time of general famine or overwhelming pestilence. But for other claims the limiting factor will not be availability but goodwill. The claim of women to equal pay or for laws against sexual harassment or discrimination can readily be met by a society that takes women seriously. The call for self-determination is about taking indigenous peoples seriously.

On not making it a guilt trip

We have it on the authority of one of our captains of industry that it is theologically incorrect to speak of guilt being transmitted from one generation to another. (Our miners are apparently bathed in the blood of a very convenient lamb at the turning point of the generations.) However, what can be transmitted from one generation to another is not guilt but debt. Generations of Australians yet unborn will carry the burden of the greed and stupidity of this generation in the matter of overseas debt. The present generation of Australians have inherited a debt of another kind.

If my uncle Silas acquired a property by fraud and deception and left it to me in his will, it would not be enough for me to have prayers said for the repose of his soul. If the circumstances of the case came to my notice, I would have to see what I should to do remedy the injustice. It might well be true that I had no part in the original injustice, but I have inherited the fruits of it, and property cries out for its owner, as the old dictum has it.

In driving the Aborigines off their land, the whites did more than deprive them of their property. They deprived them of their independence, their culture and their spiritual world. To restore to them the land that was theirs, or to acknowledge their ownership of the land they still occupy, is only to restore part of what has been taken from them.

The present generation of non-Aboriginal Australians inherit not the guilt but the liabilities of generations that have gone before, for they are the beneficiaries of their injustices. The present generation of Aborigines inherit the rights that should have been theirs in a just line of inheritance. One generation can dissipate the birthright of the generation that follows, and that is just bad luck for their heirs; but if their property or their land is unjustly taken from them, morally speaking they retain the right to it, and so do their lawful descendants.

Not just land

Our concern is not just about land rights but about everything that goes with the land in the case of indigenous peoples in general, and Australian Aborigines in particular. Naboth's vineyard was worth more to him than money, and it could not be replaced by another, better vineyard: 'The Lord forbid that I should give you the inheritance of my fathers' (1 Kings 21:3). For Aborigines land is worth more than money, and they are not interested in exchanging it for better land elsewhere—not simply out of a strong sense of family piety, as in the case of Naboth, but because it is for them the spiritual basis of their lives. It is not enough to give them land, or to recognise their title to the land they still occupy; they must be given the right to *live* their relationship to the land, and this will require the right to a degree of autonomy corresponding to the special relationship of this people to their land.

Another way of putting this is that we are not to deal with the Aborigines as though they were simply a welfare case in contemporary Australian society. They are poor for the most part, and their health standards are appalling, but this is not to be solved simply by increased funding. Their malaise is that of a people caught between two cultures. They cannot make the best of their lot in the ascendent white culture because it is not theirs, and they cannot make the best of their own culture because they are powerless and are acting out a script that has been written for them by others.

Self-determination is as important for a group as it is for an individual if the group is to have an identity and a character of its own. If that identity is already a given, as it is with a group based on racial and cultural distinctiveness, there will be an unremitting tension and frustration if that group is not allowed to shape its own destiny within the bounds of the possible. As in the case of the individual person, it is not enough that the right and beneficial decisions be taken in the person's regard, if these decisions are always taken by others. It is part of the person's flourishing as a human being that their destiny should be shaped by the exercise of their own freedom, which is the highest attribute of the human being.

The experience of freedom includes for all of us the experience of the limitations of freedom. It is necessary that we should accept limitations on our personal freedom in order that others might enjoy freedom in their turn. This is a sacrifice that we make for the common good. But the good for which the sacrifice is made is *common*, that is to say, it is shared by the members of the community who are called upon to make such sacrifices.

It is part of good government, and an exercise of what is traditionally known as *distributive justice*, that the benefits and burdens required of the citizenry be fairly distributed. It might be for the greater good of the greater number that one sector of the population be treated in an oppressive way, but this would not be justice. For example, the farming community should not be condemned to perpetual penury in order that the populations of the cities might rejoice in cheap food and have more to spend on luxuries.

The quest for justice, however, is not a matter of equal treatment for all; it will require that unequal cases are not treated equally, but are treated with due regard for the special circumstances of the case. The call for self-determination for indigenous peoples is a call for justice. To treat them as though they were the same as the later comers, whose culture proved to be the dominant one, is not fair treatment, for they are not the same, and the 'common good' to which the supervenient culture subscribes is not their good. The differences are not just economic but include the more important spiritual goods of self-understanding, social structure, customary law and religion.

To return to the definition of self determination proposed by the UN Working Group on Indigenous Populations:

> Indigenous people have the right to self-determination. By virtue of this right, they freely determine their relationship with the states in which they live, in a spirit of co-existence with other citizens, and freely pursue their economic, social, cultural and spiritual development in conditions of freedom and dignity.[6]

'They freely determine their relationship with the states in which they live.' The self-determination sought for indigenous peoples is not usually full sovereignty, though there are some Aborigines for whom nothing less than full sovereignty will suffice. Leaving aside philosophical considerations as to what is required before a community can qualify for sovereignty, there is the very practical consideration that nothing in the United Nations declarations or covenants is aimed at the breaking up of the national states that are signatory to the UN Charter, nor is any Australian government likely to consent to the secession of part of its citizenry and territory. Referring to Paul Coe's unsuccessful attempt in 1978 to get the High Court to acknowledge Aboriginal sovereignty, Frank Brennan comments that Aboriginal sovereignty is not something that can be vindicated in any Australian court or in the International Court of Justice.

> Aboriginal sovereignty is at best a political claim. By asserting the continuation of their sovereignty, Aborigines are presumably seeking a legal basis on which to exercise power over land and resources and increased control of their own lives as individuals and communities. That basis will not emerge from any court declaration of sovereignty. It may result from some parliamentary acknowledgement of Aboriginal entitlements backed by a legal machinery for recognition and enforcement.[7]

So the self-determination that the Aborigines can reasonably aspire to is less than sovereignty, and more in the nature of possibilities mentioned by Frank Brennan: 'power over land and resources, and increased control of their own lives as individuals and communities'. With such a degree of autonomy they may be in a position, in the words of the WGIP declaration, 'freely to pursue their economic, social, cultural and spiritual development in conditions of freedom and dignity'.

Local government?

It is not likely that the appropriate forms of autonomy will be found within the forms of government with which we are familiar in Australia. According to Frank Brennan:

> Aborigines committed to self-determination see the possibility of constituting themselves as another order of government in the federal structure of Australia. To date, governments have been prepared to concede local government status to Aboriginal communities. Some Aborigines argue that just as they are permitted to perform their own local government functions, so too they should be able to perform in their communities some of the services and

rules of State and Commonwealth government. They might then come to determine their future, not merely managing their present in accordance with policy directives from State and Commonwealth governments.[8]

This granted, there remains a situation of great complexity, with different groups representing different interests and having different relationships to the larger Australian society.

The complexities of the situation demand that the views of the Aborigines be carefully sought by ways of consultation that are in harmony with their culture. If justice is to be done it should be done speedily for a people who have waited 200 years for it. The process of reconciliation that is proposed for completion by the time of the centenary of Federation in the year 2001 has great symbolic value and could be at least the beginnings of a final arrangement that would respect the special status of our indigenous people. A charter is needed which would give due recognition to their culture, their claim to their land and their need for a degree of self-management. It is not within the scope of this paper to be more specific than that.

As I write, the world summit on the environment is taking place at Rio de Janeiro. Anguish is expressed at the destruction of the forests of the world and the degradation of the environment. Nothing of any lasting worth will be done until modern technological humanity learns to reverence nature and to work with it rather than dominating it and tearing it apart. Modern humankind needs the wisdom of the indigenous peoples of the world the way the ecology needs the rainforests. To give these peoples the self-determination they need in order to foster their culture and preserve their relationship with the earth is to preserve a little flame from which a future generation may kindle for itself a more serene and more enduring light.

Chapter 5

A Theological
Approach to
Reconciliation

JOHN WILCKEN SJ

It is important to state at the outset the approach I am taking in
this chapter. It is that of Christian theology. There are
considerable advantages in this. Christianity is a world-wide
missionary faith which, many times in its history, has had to
face the issue of wide cultural differences between peoples and
the resulting problems and conflicts. In practice it has not
always dealt with this issue very well. But at least the issue has
had to be faced, and one can learn from the experience of the
past.

The problem of relations between Aboriginal and non-
Aboriginal peoples could also be discussed from the stand-
point of Aboriginal religion. That would be a helpful contribution to the enterprise of moving towards reconciliation.
However, such a task is not one that I can accomplish. In this
chapter I am writing simply from the point of view of Christian
theology.

The situation and its history

First I need to recall, at least briefly, the situation upon which
we are reflecting, and give a short account of the history lying
behind it. Aborigines came to Australia many thousands of
years ago. Where they came from is not altogether clear.
Maybe, too, there were different waves of migration. In the

relatively isolated situation in which they remained for so long, they developed their culture, their particular way of living in this land. While there are cultural differences within Australia, and a plurality of languages, it is nevertheless possible to speak of *an* Australian Aboriginal culture—one that is highly developed, deeply religious, and closely associated with nature and the land. The way of life was nomadic or semi-nomadic. In the centuries just before European settlement there was some cultural contact with people from the north, especially from what is now called Indonesia.

In 1788 European settlement began, and the European population increased rapidly over the next 200 years. The culture of the Europeans was utterly foreign to that of the original inhabitants, and mutual understanding was difficult. The Europeans were vastly more advanced technologically, and they simply took possession of the land, beginning with the more fertile areas, developing it according to the methods they knew. In the clashes that inevitably occurred with the Aborigines into whose lands they were intruding, there was violence and bloodshed on both sides. However, the technological superiority of the Europeans ensured that they were successful. What can be termed massacres of the Aboriginal population occurred. Moreover, wherever Aborigines and Europeans had some continuing contact with each other, the terms of the relationship were determined, consciously or unconsciously, by the Europeans. They assumed that their 'superior' culture was to prevail. It was in fact anticipated by many Europeans that the Aborigines would eventually die out—as they did in Tasmania. Some Aborigines did try to adapt creatively to the situation, for example by attempting to incorporate Europeans into their kinship relationships. But the Europeans in general were quite ignorant of Aboriginal ways, and did not think that their customs, beliefs and practices were worth bothering about.

An Aboriginal population survives today, but as a depressed group in the community, with a standard of living in general much lower than that of the dominant, non-Aboriginal population, and with limited opportunities to 'make good' in Australian society. Much of Aboriginal culture and language has been lost. In remote parts of Australia there are efforts to preserve the traditional life, but the considerable numbers of urban Aborigines are largely cut off from their cultural roots.

Land and the landscape are of central importance to Aboriginal culture; yet, to a large extent, the European population has taken over the land, establishing legal title to it according to its own laws. The Aborigines are largely dispossessed of their land, yet their very identity as Aborigines has traditionally been bound up with the land and their relationship to it.

Culture

What has happened in Australia is that two vastly different cultures have come in contact, and in conflict, with each other. Culture is enormously important for the growth and identity of the individual. We are the people we are largely because of the culture we began to absorb and make our own from the very beginning of our individual life. The way we see the world, the values we live by, the defences we set up against threatening forces in the world around us and in our own nature, the means we use to affirm ourselves and to make progress in our society—all this, and much more, is largely culturally determined.

Cultural traditions, which have developed through centuries and millennia of human experience, enable us to live in a human way, with dignity, self-respect and basic security. It is hard to separate individuals from their culture, so deeply is it ingrained in them. A person's sense of identity is closely linked with his or her culture.

Injustice

When one looks at the history of Aboriginal-European relations over the last 200 years, and at the present situation, one has to acknowledge that great injustice has been done, primarily by European peoples against Aborigines. There has been first of all the seizure of the lands previously occupied by Aborigines; and since Aboriginal culture is so closely linked with the land, this has not been just a matter of taking someone else's possessions, but it has involved the virtual destruction of Aboriginal life and culture. The European settlers who took possession of the land were no doubt unaware of the extent of the injustice they were committing; but this does not alter the objective evil of what was done. Then there were all the crimes of violence, especially of Europeans against Aborigines—all the blood that was spilt. Finally there has been the continued cultural imperialism of the Europeans, which has robbed the Aborigines of their dignity, their culture, their spirituality—and, indeed, almost their identity. The result of all this is the depressed situation of Aborigines in Australia today.

Sin

In theological terms one must describe this as a sin-stained history, and the present situation as a sinful one. No doubt the word 'sin' is most commonly understood in terms of individual wrong-doing and the disorder of life that is its consequence. Sin is opposed to love, promotes disharmony and sets people at odds with each other. Sin alienates from God. Sin destroys and kills, or at least limits growth.

But sin is not found only in the lives and actions of individual human beings; it is also structured into societies and affects the history of peoples. Such structural sin is unfortunately quite common. Slavery, for example, which has existed in many human societies, is objectively wrong and contrary to human dignity. A society which accepts slavery is a sinful society, even though many individual people living in that society may be generous, loving and conscientious. Similarly a racist society is a sinful society, as is a society in which women are denied dignity and the freedom to be themselves. Great inequality of wealth and power, whether within countries or between countries, also manifests the existence of structural sin.

To return to our present concern: one has to say that sin is structured into Australian society, and has been since 1788. What might be described as the primal (or original) sin of the Australian people is the injustice done by the European settlers to the original inhabitants of this continent. This has damaged both the Aborigines and the later settlers.

The harm sustained by the European people is not so obvious as that done to the Aborigines, but is real nevertheless: there has been a hardening of hearts and a narrowing of vision, a diminishment of the capacity to share life and joy, a focusing on preserving positions of power and on accumulating material wealth—as well as the immense loss that comes from the lack of good relations with people who have much to offer in cultural richness, warmth of heart and a deeply spiritual approach to life.

Of course, side by side with this history of sin, a history of grace has also been unfolding. Much good has been done by people of both European and Aboriginal descent throughout the last 200 years. Genuine friendship has existed between individual Aborigines and Europeans, manifesting the grace of God in the midst of a sin-stained history. This has opened up possibilities of life and growth and hope. People have worked to establish structures which might improve the relationships between the white settlers and the original inhabitants—though their efforts may often have been more well-intentioned than successful. And, with regard to the injustices that have been committed, no doubt these were often the result of ignorance, or arose from actions done in moments of stress and anxiety.

However, despite these manifestations of grace, and despite the diminished culpability—and even lack of culpability—for many unjust actions, it is nevertheless true that something has gone badly wrong in Australian society, and individuals, often contrary to their best intentions, have been caught up in the evil of it all.

This can look like an irredeemable, hopeless situation. Yet Christianity is essentially about redemption and hope, and this hope is focused not only on the next world: Christian faith calls also for changes in this world, changes which can lead to the building of a more just society here and now.

Moreover, the Christian understanding of what has happened in the past, and of the situation existing in the present, has a radical and surprising quality about it. God does not see things the way human beings see them (see Isaiah 55:6-9; Mark 8:31-33); and God can bring good out of evil (Isaiah 53; Luke 18:9-14). Let us look at some aspects of our sin-stained history, and our present unjust society, in the light of the Christian faith.

God and the oppressed

One theme that appears fairly constantly in both Old and New Testaments is that God is very specially with the poor and the oppressed. In the Book of Exodus God hears the cries of his oppressed people and calls Moses from the burning bush, in order to rescue the Israelites from their life of slavery (Exodus 3). Psalm 34 speaks of God being near to the broken-hearted. According to Luke's gospel, chapter 2, Jesus was born in a stable, in what might be called a situation of real destitution. In a striking parable, Jesus spoke of the poor Lazarus, sitting at the gate of the rich man, his sores licked by dogs, who after his death was received into Abraham's bosom (Luke 16:19-31). Jesus himself died as a crucified criminal. The message comes through strongly that God is found in a special way among the poor and the oppressed, among the afflicted and the broken-hearted.

Applying this to the Australian situation one comes to the conclusion that God is found in a special way in the Aborigines, precisely in their affliction and oppression. God hears their cry, and it is God's will that they be rescued from their present plight.

Moreover, just as Jesus, in a mysterious way, proclaimed the message of God from the stable and the cross, so the Aborigines, because of their situation, speak the message of

God to the European population of Australia. It is a strange Christian paradox: the voice of the powerless is the voice of God. The non-Aboriginal population will be spiritually enriched and led to God by listening to the original inhabitants of this land. God reverses our ordinary human way of seeing things. It is not from the position of power that God's word is spoken; rather, it is spoken through the lives of the powerless.

Forgiveness

Australian history is sin-stained, and the present situation of our society is unjust. To accept that statement is, in the Christian view, to take a large step towards the healing of the hurt that has been done and the building of a more just society.

Past history is a fact, and it cannot be changed. The crimes of the last two centuries have to be owned by Australians—not as if we are personally guilty of what was done by our predecessors, but rather as acknowledging that our present situation (which includes very particularly the dominant position of the European population) stands in continuity with that sin-stained past, and is the direct result of it. Thus we Australians today cannot say that what was done in the past is no concern of ours. As people living in history, we bear the burden of the crimes of the past—just as we are enriched by the grace which was present also in the lives of our predecessors. True reconciliation can come about only if we humbly and honestly accept that burden.

Christian faith assures us that forgiveness and healing are freely available to those whose hearts are open to receive them. The crucifix, the central symbol of Christianity, is the pledge of this. Christ entered into the darkness and violence of human history, suffered their destructive power in his own body, and thereby, in a fundamental way, overcame them. The body nailed to the cross is the guarantee of God's acceptance of our world, in all its reality, and of God's forgiveness of all that needs forgiving. As St Paul says, Christ 'was given up for our sins and raised for our justification' (Romans 4:25). A fundamental redemption from all the evil of the world was brought about through Christ's crucifixion and resurrection. The forgiveness that was offered did not minimise the evil done. This evil was plumbed to its depths, and thus the forgiveness and healing are radical and total.

Acceptance of this forgiveness for the crimes of our history—not that we personally committed them, but we are part of the historical movement in which they occurred—this acceptance necessarily involves a real change of heart. The injustices of the present, which result from those past crimes, can no longer be simply tolerated or ignored. Accepting forgiveness means responding to the call to work, in whatever way we can, to improve the situation of both Aboriginal and other Australians (since injustices imposed on one section of the population cause damage, in some way, to all, as has been explained above). Thus acceptance of forgiveness, far from causing gloom and hopelessness, brings energy and initiative and the desire to work for a better future. New life can spring up when we own our history in the spirit of faith.

New Life

An example of the new life that can emerge following the acceptance of forgiveness is given in Luke's account of the extraordinary union of minds and hearts among the early Christians, to the extent that they shared their goods among each other and held all things in common (Acts 4:32-37). No doubt this is a rather idealised picture of Christian origins, but it does emphasise the radical change in human relationships that results from faith in Jesus and acceptance of forgiveness through his death and resurrection (see Acts 2:22-42). A change somewhat along these lines is called for in the matter of relationships between Aborigines and other people in Australia. The basis for reconciliation is the unlimited divine forgiveness which is accepted through faith and brings a real conversion of heart; out of this comes hope, and the spirit of love leads to positive action for better relationships.

Culture and the New Testament

Let us return to the theme of culture. Jesus of Nazareth grew up in a village in Galilee, learning and adopting the culture of his own Jewish people. Since he was fully human, this Jewish culture became an integral part of his earthly life. He was humanly enriched by this culture, but in time became critical of some aspects of it, such as its emphasis on externals in religious behaviour (e.g. Mark 7:1-23). As he came to insist on interior rightness of heart and such basic virtues as justice, mercy and love (e.g. Matthew 23:23-24 and Mark 12:28-34), he made his message of peace and hope less dependent on a particular cultural tradition and more open to being embodied and incarnated in any culture.

The test of this openness to other cultures came after his death and resurrection, when the saving power of his life, death and resurrection came to be preached to non-Jews. Then the question arose as to whether circumcision and the Mosaic Law had to be imposed on Gentiles as a precondition for their becoming Christians. The answer given by the early Church was that these preconditions were not required (Acts 15, Galatians 2:1-10). Thus it was declared that all cultures were open to Christianity, and one could be a Greek Christian or an Ethiopian Christian and so on, as well as a Jewish Christian. Christianity was not limited to those of Jewish culture. The basic goodness of all cultures was affirmed. Yet, since culture is a human construction, and thus shares human imperfection, Christianity will also have a purifying effect on all the cultures in which it is incarnated (see Vatican II, *Dogmatic Constitution on the Church*, nos 13 and 17).

Since our culture is such a deep and integral part of us, the situation can easily arise where people tend to see an indissoluble link between their culture and their Christian faith. This happened in the very early Church when, in spite of the decision not to impose Jewish customs on Gentile converts, there was continuing friction between Christian Jews and Christian Gentiles. The problem became acute in Antioch, and Peter and Paul publicly disagreed on the best way of dealing with the situation (Galatians 2:11-21). It became one of the great tasks of Paul's life to bring it about that his Gentile converts throughout the Mediterranean world would be fully accepted as Christian brothers and sisters by the Jewish Christian community of Jerusalem. This seems to have been the main reason for his money-raising venture among the Christian communities he had founded in various cities of the Roman Empire, and his plan to bring the money he had collected to the Jewish Christians in Jerusalem (e.g. see Romans 15:25-33). It is not quite clear how successful this effort at reconciliation was, but it proved costly to Paul personally, resulting in years of imprisonment for him (see Acts, chapters 21 to 28).

The problem of too close an identification of Christianity with a particular culture is constantly with us, and is shown, for example, in the way missionaries from Europe tended to bring to the peoples of Asia, Africa and the Americas a specifically European form of Christianity—and, indeed, to impose such a form of Christianity on converted peoples. Yet fundamentally Christianity is open to all cultures, and its inner dynamism calls for it to be incarnated in each different culture.

Cultures in Australia

To turn to the Australian scene, Christianity is, of itself, open both to European-style culture and to Aboriginal-style culture—and indeed, affirms the essential goodness of each tradition (and, of course, of all the other traditions in our multicultural society). Yet the inner dynamism of Christianity is also to be a purifying and elevating influence in each culture. All cultures have their human limitations, and there can be dehumanising elements in each cultural tradition. Thus Europeans may look at Aboriginal ways and be critical, for example, of the harshness of some practices, such as sub-incision. Aborigines may look at twentieth century European history and see the massive defects of a way of life that has led to two World Wars, the development of weapons of mass destruction, a genocidal attack on the Jewish people in the Nazi period, and the endangering of the survival of life on the planet through ecological irresponsibility. The Christian message challenges and criticises each cultural tradition.

Conflict of cultures

Let us return to the question of the conflict between Aboriginal culture and European culture in Australia. A decisive factor in the situation has been the technological superiority of Europeans, which has meant that power has been in their hands. Hence they have succeeded in establishing their way of life, at the cost of the large-scale destruction of the Aboriginal lifestyle. Fertile country is now occupied by grainfields and by flocks of sheep and herds of cattle. Mining industries gouge out coal and minerals from the earth. Rivers are harnessed for irrigation and hydro-electric power. The building of dams means the flooding of land. Forests are cut down. White people's laws have regulated the life of the population. White people's political bodies have made the significant decisions. Advancement in Australian society can take place only by passing through the white people's educational system, and so on. This cultural imperialism (no doubt often unconsciously and inculpably carried on) has devastated Aboriginal society. And Aboriginal spirituality and religion are so closely linked to the land and the natural contours of the landscape that the spirituality of the Aborigines has suffered greatly.

This means that individual Aborigines are gravely disadvantaged. The bases of their self-confidence are eroded. Life may scarcely seem worth living at times. The widespread alcoholism, the large numbers of Aborigines in prison, and the number of deaths in custody bear witness to a loss of hope among Aborigines.

Christ in the needy

In Matthew's gospel, chapter 25, occurs the powerful story of the gathering together of all the nations before the Son of Man, who separates them from one another as a shepherd separates sheep from goats. The words addressed by the King to those assembled before him could be paraphrased for our situation in words such as these:

I was dispossessed of my own land, which was part of my very being ...

I was uprooted from my cultural heritage ...

I was deprived of my religious traditions and spirituality ...

I was taken as a child from my parents and family ...

I was regarded as ignorant, incompetent and irrespons‐ ible ...

I was hunted like a kangaroo ...

I was imprisoned for drunkenness ...

And so on. No doubt the European settlers could also make up a similar list of possible sayings of the Lord appropriate to them. Yet the burden of need has certainly weighed more heavily on the Aborigines. Thus it is with them that Christ more especially identifies himself, asking people how they have responded to their needs.

Structural change

Individuals live in structured societies, and thus, if the welfare of individuals is to be promoted in any lasting fashion, social structures have to be changed, so as to give people greater freedom to be themselves and to make possible a more equita‐ ble sharing of the benefits—both material and spiritual—of society.

The structures involved here are not only the external ones of political institutions, the economic system, law en‐ forcement, the education system and so on, but also the inner structures of mind of the population: attitudes, viewpoints, prejudices, popular beliefs, suspicions, fears, and the like. A conversion of heart is frequently needed if these inner structures are to be changed. There can scarcely be any lasting and effective improvement at the level of external institutions if there is no appropriate modification of the inner structures of the minds and hearts of people.

Power

A key factor in the achievement of structural change is that of power. The European population has a monopoly of power in Australian society, and the Aborigines are basically powerless. Such an imbalance of power cannot be the basis for a healthy and just society.

Here is where the message of Jesus of Nazareth makes its most radical demands: in order that there may be a proper distribution of power in our society, the European population needs to take positive steps to *dispossess* itself of power. This is something people find extremely difficult to do, yet Jesus both preached this message, and gave examples of it in his own life.

In Matthew 4:1-11 Jesus was tempted to make use of power in several ways, and refused to do so: he did not change the stones into bread; he did not cast himself down from the pinnacle of the Temple, confident that he would be borne up by angels; he did not accept kingship of the whole world. Later, when the crowd wanted to make him king after the feeding of the multitude, he escaped from them and went up the mountain by himself (John 6:15). In the beatitudes, which especially express the radicalism of his message, he spoke of poverty, meekness, mercy, peace-making, being persecuted (Matthew 5:1-12). At the Last Supper he washed the feet of his disciples (John 13:1-15). Above all, he was captured in Jerusalem and crucified, dying in utter powerlessness. Both by word and example Jesus proclaimed that the way of powerlessness is the way of God.

This is not an easy message to receive and act upon in public life in Australia, or in any other human society. Yet if reconciliation between Aborigines and others is to be achieved, *some* dispossession of power on the part of the latter is essential. The Gospel proclaimed by Jesus calls for such a way of proceeding.

Vision

People of vision are needed if lasting and worthwhile changes are to take place. Somehow the imagination of the population needs to be touched, and the possibilities for the future presented with a real sense of hope and confidence. Jesus was a visionary in this sense, and he expressed his vision in terms of a traditional Jewish concept: the Reign of God (e.g. Mark 1:15). Somehow, through the power of God, the world would be changed. God's justice and love would direct all things, and the beginnings of such a transformation would occur even in this life. Jesus died for that vision, and he bequeathed it to his followers so that they might continue to proclaim it and embody it in their own personal lives.

We need a vision of what Australian society can become: a vision which will make concrete and specific for this country what Jesus was proclaiming in his own time through the phrase, the Reign of God. It is not a slogan that is being asked for—there are plenty of those around. Nor do we want a presentation of what simply suits the interests of one group in our society. What is needed is a vision which expresses God's hopes for our land, and it will include a call for justice, love, peace and reconciliation. Maybe poets and artists have to make their contribution here, as well as civic and religious leaders. But we do need a vision.

Some conclusions

What I have written is primarily for the people of this country who are not Aboriginal, especially those of European descent. Hence, to draw together what I have been presenting in this chapter I will set out what seems to be required of European

Australians if there is to be a genuine movement towards reconciliation:

• to own the reality of Australian history, especially of the last 200 years; to appreciate at depth what has happened; to see the way this sin-stained history largely determines our present situation;

• to recognise that God speaks in a special way through the Aborigines of Australia;

• to accept forgiveness for the evil that has been done and to be open to the new life that can emerge;

• to halt, as far as possible, the continuing imperialism of the technologically superior European culture;

• to take real steps towards an active self-dispossession of power;

• and to do this in the light of a vision for the future which is in harmony with God's hopes for our country.

Chapter 6

Home-Coming:
Scriptural Reflections upon a
Process of Reconciliation

BRENDAN BYRNE SJ

The theme of wandering, being on a journey, is pervasive in the Jewish-Christian scriptures. From the call of Abraham onwards there appears the quest to arrive at and to possess the promised land. The image has entered the Christian tradition as a standard metaphor of the life of faith.

Possession of the land may be a central motif in scripture. But with respect to it there is also room for hesitation. The biblical book of Joshua reports and celebrates Israel's conquest of the land of Canaan. For Israel this conquest is the fulfilment of promises made to the ancestors of the nation, the final act in the great drama of liberation that began with the exodus from Egypt. For the people already living in the land, the Canaanites, it meant slaughter, loss and dispossession. Within the Australian context, one cannot help seeing the original inhabitants of this land cast in the role of the hapless Canaanites whom Israel dispossessed, seemingly at the behest of God.[1]

Whether any of the white settlers who took possession of Australia from 1788 onwards explicitly appealed to Joshua in justification of their act, I do not know. Certainly, this did happen in the case of other colonisations.[2] Such an arrogant and wrongheaded use of scripture hardly needs refutation today. Here is a case where a biblical motif has virtually to be inverted in order to conform to the wider framework of the gospel.

Clearly, then, a scriptural reflection on reconciliation between Aborigines and other Australians must proceed with great sensitivity to such issues. It is for the original inhabitants themselves to say what meaning they find in scriptural texts read from their own situation. Oppressed peoples in the world, especially in Latin America, Black Northern America and Asia, have found in the central Old Testament motif of the Exodus a paradigm powerfully addressing their own plight and hopes for liberation. I see no reason why Aboriginal Australian Christians should not also own it in similar terms. But this I shall leave to them. It is for the oppressed, those who are 'inside' the experience, to be the first to give expression to its contemporary meaning.

My own perspective is that of a white Australian reflecting biblically upon the situation in which we Australians who are not Aboriginal find ourselves today. We have a land. We dwell for the most part on its fertile rim, fascinated by its harsh yet strangely beautiful interior. But we do not truly possess this land; nor are we fully at home within it. An ambiguity hovers over our tenure—the moral and spiritual ambiguity of a conquest that is physical but not yet fully human. Our holding has yet to come to terms fully with the manner of its taking: that our possession meant radical and usually bloody dispossession of those here long before us. A subtle alienation will subvert our tenure of this land so long as we do not own this truth and seek, in reconciliation, to remedy its lingering effects.

What I propose to do from here on is to consider the call to reconciliation in the light of six leading areas of the New Testament: the four gospels (Matthew, Mark, Luke and John), the Pauline letters and the letter to the Hebrews. Not all of these texts treat specifically the theme of 'reconciliation'. But each makes its own distinctive challenge to the task that lies before us.

Matthew

The central aim of Matthew is to promote the higher justice of
the Kingdom. The language of 'justice' (or 'righteousness')
stems from Jewish tradition, which Matthew is very much
concerned to preserve, while also insisting upon the newness
of what had come about through Jesus. The law (*torah*) of
Moses required 'righteousness' of human beings in the sense
of fulfilment of God's will expressed in its commands. The
new law promulgated by Jesus also requires righteousness, but
a deeper, more radical righteousness, which he himself both
models and teaches.

Six blocks of teaching appearing early in Jesus' Sermon
on the Mount (5:21-48) inculcate this new righteousness. Each
is set in the form of an antithesis to show both continuity and
contrast between the old way and the new.

The first (5:21-26) takes up the prohibition given to
'those of old': 'Thou shalt not kill, ... whoever kills shall be
liable to judgment'. Jesus both radicalises and generalises the
issue: 'I say to you, if you are angry with a brother or a sister
you shall be liable to judgment'. The new righteousness ex-
cludes not merely the external action (killing) but even the
hostile disposition.

Jesus then pursues the matter into the more strictly
religious sphere:

> So when you are offering your gift at the altar, and there remem-
> ber that your brother or sister has something against you, leave
> your gift there before the altar and go; first be reconciled to your
> brother or sister, and then come and offer your gift (5:23-24).

Here we have a subtle shift in perspective. It is not a
hostile disposition on the part of the offerer that is now the
problem. It is rather a sense that someone—brother or sister—
has something against *me*. Lack of mutual reconciliation on
the human plane creates a barrier to acceptance by God.

Jesus speaks here in the line of the great prophets of Israel, as, for example, Isaiah:

> What to me is the multitude of your sacrifices?
> says the Lord;
> I have had enough of burnt offerings of rams
>   and the fat of fed beasts ...
> Your new moons and your appointed feasts
>   my soul hates;
> they have become a burden to me,
>   I am weary of bearing them.
> Wash yourselves; make yourselves clean;
>   remove the evil of your doings
>   from before my eyes.
> Cease to do evil; learn to do good.
> Seek justice, correct oppression;
> defend the fatherless, plead for the widow ...
> Though your sins are like scarlet,
>   they shall be as white as snow;
> though they are red like crimson,
>   they shall become like wool (Isaiah 1:11-20).

Likewise Amos:

> I hate, I despise your feasts,
>   and I take no delight in your solemn assemblies ...
> But let justice roll down like waters,
>   and righteousness like an ever-flowing stream (5:21-24).

Resuming this prophetic complaint, Jesus makes reconciliation with one's fellow human beings an essential precondition of true worship—part of that deeper righteousness characteristic of the kingdom.

The following lines continue the same idea from a somewhat different perspective:

> Make friends quickly with your accuser, while you are going with him to court, lest your accuser hand you over to the judge, and the judge to the guard, and you be put in prison; truly, I say to you, you will never get out till you have paid the last penny (5:25-26).

The sense now is not so much of approaching God in worship as of being found unreconciled at the coming judgment, a theme never far from sight in Matthew (see 11:20-24; 13:24-30, 36-43, 47-50; 22:11-14; 25:31-46). The incredible gift of the Kingdom and the acceptance of the sinner which it involves does not remove final accountability to God.

Outside the Pauline letters, this text of Matthew is the only place where the New Testament speaks explicitly of reconciliation. It does so in a highly significant context (the Sermon on the Mount) where Jesus indicates what is truly characteristic of Christian life and responsibility. Australian Christians, conscious of the hurt carried by Koori brothers and sisters, cannot lightly dismiss the challenge of his words.

Mark

A striking feature of Mark's gospel is the way in which Jesus appears from the start in conflict with the demonic (1:21-28, 32-34; 3:11-12; 5:1-20; 7:24-30; 9:14-29). The pervasiveness of this feature in Mark raises problems for modern interpretation. The ancient worldview attributed to demons conditions and illnesses now seen as forms of mental or physical illness. But rather than dismiss this worldview altogether, I would urge that we attend to the full scope of the demonic in Mark and note the sophistication with which it is handled.

The demonic in Mark is essentially about control—the subtle control of human life exercised by unseen, supra-personal forces; these alienate human beings from God and from their own true humanity. Pitched against these forces, Jesus proclaims and enacts the freedom associated with the Kingdom (1:14-15). He is the 'Stronger One', who comes to 'bind the Strong Man' (Satan) and 'burgle his house' (3:27).

What soon becomes clear as the gospel proceeds is that the demonic with which Jesus is in conflict is not confined to overt cases of possession. It is at work also in the resistance and ultimate hostility of the religious leaders, who see in Jesus a rival and threat to their hold upon the people. Jesus' teaching is a real exorcism of ignorance and despair. The people note that he teaches 'with authority, not like the scribes' (1:22). The implication is that sabbath after sabbath the demonic had lived comfortably alongside conventional religion. Jesus, in sharp contrast, presents a liberating challenge.

More subtly still, however, the demonic is at work also in the hearts of Jesus' own disciples. The entire drama revolves around their struggles, and ultimate failure to come to terms with the emerging truth that Jesus will complete his mission in suffering and death, rather than messianic triumph. The key paradigm of their failure comes midway through the gospel in the exchange between Jesus and Simon Peter at Caesarea Philippi. Peter, on hearing Jesus' first prophecy of his passion and death, takes him aside and begins to remonstrate with him, earning the sharp rebuke, 'Get behind me, Satan' (8:33). The disciples' fear and unwillingness to comprehend show that they too lie in some degree under the control of Satan.

Recognising the pervasiveness of the demonic in Mark means going beyond seeing Jesus as ministering simply to individual distress. The opposition to Jesus is transpersonal and structural; it concerns all those forces and powers, with their attendant myths and deceits, that alienate and stunt human life across the broadest possible spectrum.[3] The gospel invites us to write in, as it were, the demons of our own time; to question ourselves rigorously and seriously concerning manifestations of the demonic today: the arms-race, the manipulation of capital, racial prejudice, religious and social fundamentalism, the quest for security at all cost? The list could go on indefinitely, embracing all that deceptively yet effectively controls human life, stunting growth, harmony and freedom.

The chilling contribution of Mark's gospel is its suggestion—and more than a suggestion—that the demonic is not necessarily confined to groups outside the believing community. The fear and obstinacy of the disciples becomes a major hindrance to the mission of Jesus, who can only exorcise the evil in the world by entering into its pain and suffering in obedience to God's will. In this way Mark challenges believers to ask constantly whether a religious belief that has become comfortable has not also become blind and hence an obstacle, rather than an aid, to the saving work of God.

Mark's Jesus is the great boundary breaker, the one who insists that holiness is defined by God's presence, rather than by rules or boundaries delimiting holy persons, things, and places. Mark challenges us to ask where God dwells in our community. In well-run parish communities, churches and schools? Undoubtedly. But the holy presence of God is there also in the margins—in the suffering and alienated whose situation most mirrors that of Jesus dying upon the cross, mocked by his co-religionists, seemingly abandoned by his God and yet, as the resurrection will show, the real focus of God's presence and power (15:29-39). It is the pagan centurion, the supervisor of the execution, who alone admits what no one else can see: that this condemned outlaw is truly the Son of God (v. 39). Mark's gospel suggests that our eyes may have to be opened, the demons in our own hearts exorcised, if we are to be free enough to share his vision of God's ways.

Luke

Jesus inaugurates his public ministry in Luke's gospel with a 'programmatic' sermon in the synagogue of his home town, Nazareth (4:16-30). He begins by quoting a celebrated passage from Isaiah 61 (vv. 1-2) where the prophet describes his commissioning by the Spirit to proclaim the good news of liberation. Having read the verses and handed back the scroll to the attendant, Jesus solemnly announces, '*Today* this scripture has been fulfilled in your hearing' (v. 21). In the presence of Jesus and the message he proclaims the long-awaited salvation has arrived.

Jesus quotes Isaiah 61:1-2 in the following way:

> The Spirit of the Lord is upon me,
> because he has anointed me
> to preach good news to the poor.

He has sent me to proclaim release to the captives
   and recovering of sight to the blind,
     to set at liberty those who are oppressed,
to proclaim the acceptable year of the Lord.

    The quotation does not reproduce the text of Isaiah exactly. It retains from the original the motif of 'good news for the poor' and the reference to 'release for captives'. It also keeps the proclamation of 'a year of acceptance from the Lord'—an opportunity for reconciliation—but drops a less positive allusion to 'a day of vengeance'. More significantly, Luke has Jesus add a phrase that does not occur in Isaiah 61 at all but comes from a slightly earlier passage in the same book (58:6). This phrase, 'to set at liberty those who are oppressed', adds to the text a further 'freedom' reference. In fact, in its original context the prophet, speaking in God's name, makes carrying out the demands of social justice the true way of fulfilling a fast:

Is not this the fast that I choose:
   to loose the bonds of wickedness,
   to undo the thongs of the yoke,
to let the oppressed go free,
   and to break every yoke?
Is it not to share your bread with the hungry,
   and bring the homeless poor into your house;
when you see the naked, to cover him,
   and not to hide yourself from your own flesh? (58:6-7)

    That is, Jesus' own mission of evangelisation seeks to implement the programme of social justice which, according to Isaiah, God required of Israel. Liberation of the oppressed has become a central element of the gospel. In this respect the 'programmatic' statement in Luke 4:16-20 is of a piece with the general tendency in Luke to stress the social aspect of the gospel. Salvation is not something confined to an otherworldly future state. It begins here and now when certain social patterns are realised in everyday human life.

One key pattern, perhaps the dominant one in Luke, occurs when outsiders—those on the margins—are brought in and made central. This, for Luke, illustrates the inclusive power of God's grace. Instanced many times in the gospel, it appears most clearly and simply in the Zaccheus episode in Luke 19 (vv. 1-10).

Zaccheus, a senior tax-collector, is by definition an outsider—one excluded by his trade from true citizenship in the people of God. He wants to see Jesus but his diminutive stature and the press of the crowd force him into the comical ploy of climbing a tree. Jesus, however, draws this outsider into the centre, summoning him down from his tree and expressing the intention of dining at his house. The proposal draws universal complaint. But Zaccheus defends himself stoutly: 'The half my goods I give to the poor and if I have defrauded any one of anything, I restore it fourfold' (v. 8). These words are usually taken as a token of conversion on Zaccheus' part: that he has resolved to amend his ways for the future. But in the Greek original Zaccheus' words do not connote conversion; they refer to his present practice, not his future policy.[4] The gospel in fact makes no judgment on the morality of Zaccheus' trade nor on his interior state. What is central for Luke is the fact that the outsider has been brought within the community ('he too is a son of Abraham') and it is precisely in terms of this transformation of social patterns that 'salvation' is defined, 'Today (that is, here and now) salvation has come to this house' (v. 9).

Elsewhere in Luke's gospel, particularly in Mary's *Magnificat* (1:46-55) and the Beatitudes (6:20-26), salvation also entails reversal of current values and social patterns. But the Zaccheus episode, with its ability to illustrate graphically the 'outsider/insider' transformation and to define salvation is those terms, makes a powerful address to Christians conscious that the one group most notably on the margins of Australian society is the Aboriginal community. Can we speak of the 'dawning' of salvation in our society until this pattern has been reversed? Luke would, I suspect, not enquire into rights and wrongs, into who is deserving and who not. He would simply indicate that, so long as the outsiders remain outside and their privileged sense of God ('Blessed are the poor ...') is not in some sense normative, the 'Today' of salvation has yet to arrive.

John

At first sight, John's gospel would seem to be the least applicable to social issues. The life of the community and the relationship of the individual believer to Jesus stand at the forefront of its concern. But the core focus of the Fourth Gospel lies upon the gift of life, the 'more abundant' life communicated to human beings by Jesus as agent of the Father (10:10; 20:31). In the course of the gospel Jesus' commission to give life becomes very much an aggressive conflict with forces making for death.[5] To use the imagery of the gospel, 'The light shines in the darkness and the darkness has not been able to master it' (1:5).

In effect, Jesus communicates life to the world only by giving up his own life. Bringing human beings to that fullness of life and humanity which is God's design for them ('eternal life') exacts a severe cost in social terms. Thus the gospel does not move entirely on the private plane. It sharply addresses issues of power and resistance in human society.

These issues come strikingly to the fore in the episode of the raising of Jesus' friend Lazarus (John 11:1-54). The remarkable restoration of Lazarus to ordinary physical life acts as a symbol of the 'eternal life' held out to all believers.[6] But it threatens the hold over the people exercised by the ruling authorities. They argue: 'If we let him go on thus, every one will come to believe in him, and the Romans will come and destroy both our holy place and our nation' (v. 48). So it seems better, 'that one man [Jesus] should die for the people' (v. 29).

There is no resurrection, no giving of life in a world alienated from God, without conflict and cost.

The gospel probes this human resistance to the gift of life in several ways. It constantly asks why, when the light of life appears, human beings prefer to stay in the darkness and in effect strike back at the light (see 1:9-11; 3:19-21; 8:40; 9:39-41; 12:46-47). It suggests that they do so for fear that their deeds will be revealed. They refuse in this sense to 'come to the truth', the truth about God and reality of the world as revealed by Jesus. To 'come to the truth' involves a total conversion, one so radical that Jesus can only describe it to Nicodemus in terms of being 'reborn' or born 'from above' (3:3-8).

The trial before Pilate (18:28 – 19:16) is the centre-piece of the passion of Jesus according to John. Here we find another individual struggling to 'come to the truth'. Pilate knows that Jesus is innocent but cannot act on this truth because it threatens his own authority. So he utters history's most famous throwaway line, 'What is truth?' and returns to fruitless argument with the Jewish leaders (18:38). Instead of coming to the truth, the truth that would make him free (8:32), he is trapped in his fear of offending Caesar and so losing whatever power he wields (19:12).

In contrast to Pilate, the gospel presents us with figures such as the Man Born Blind (9:1-41) and the Samaritan Woman (4:5-42) who do come to the light and to the truth as revealed in Jesus. In the dialogue with the woman Jesus points to a coming worship of the Father 'in spirit and in truth' (4:23), which will overcome the age-old community division between Jews and Samaritans. It is not a question of one tradition simply taking over the other. On the contrary, while acknowledging the priority of Jerusalem (v. 22), Jesus dialogues with the Samaritan tradition in the person of the woman and gently leads her to be the evangeliser of her own people. In allowing Jesus to disclose the story of her own life (vv. 16-19), in so 'coming to the truth', she becomes the archetypal worshipper of the Father in spirit and in truth, in this way bridging the religious divide. The same Fourth Gospel puts insistently to Australian Christians the question of what 'coming to the truth' might mean. Might it not involve facing up to the painful history of massacre and oppression of Aborigines that lies deep within the history of the last two hundred years? Are we truly worshipping the Father 'in spirit and in truth' if this part of the truth is not allowed to come to life? Can we really be 'free' in the Johannine sense until this truth is owned? The story of the Samaritan woman whose 'coming to the truth' broke the barrier between two alienated communities, might serve as a paradigm for the reconciliation between the two communities that sit in uneasy and unequal relationship in our own land.

Paul

As mentioned earlier, the Pauline letters provide the only extended treatment of reconciliation in the New Testament. Central to Paul's vision is what God has done for human beings in the death and resurrection of Jesus Christ. To the explanation of that divine work he brings many images, among them that of reconciliation. In a celebrated passage in 2 Corinthians he writes: 'God was in Christ reconciling the world to himself and he has entrusted to us the announcement of that reconciliation' (v. 18).

Paul draws his 'reconciliation' language from the world of diplomacy. The presupposition is that, prior to Christ, a state of hostility and alienation exists between God and human beings. Of themselves human beings can do nothing to escape from this plight. But God, in a unique act of one-sided generosity, has moved to break the impasse, effectively overcoming the hostility. The result is that those who respond in faith to the offer of reconciliation obtain 'peace with God' (Romans 5:1); like envoys of a previously hostile but now reconciled power they enjoy 'access' and welcome in God's court (v. 2).

This reconciliation has not, however, come cheaply.

There has been a cost: the cost of the suffering and death of God's own Son (Romans 5:10-11). Paul, in fact, never speaks of reconciliation save in connection with the costly shedding of Jesus' blood. For Christ reconciliation has meant bearing in his own flesh the wound and legacy of sin. Alienated from God and from life, human beings struck back at the envoy of love, nailing him at last to a cross. For believers, the resurrection is the sign and pledge that the victory rests with God's love; grace has turned hostility into reconciliation and new life.

Christ's generous act upon the cross has, then, laid the basis for a total reconciliation between human beings and their Creator. But the process is not complete. Every human life, every human structure is marked by sin; in each, both the offer and the process of reconciliation must run its course. Paul sees himself and his companions as ministers of this reconciliation offered to all (2 Corinthians 5:18 – 6:2). And this ministry, like the reconciliation it proclaims, is not achieved without cost. 'At all times', says Paul, 'we bear about in our own bodies the doing-to-death of Jesus' (4:10).

For Paul himself the process of reconciliation is 'vertical', in the sense that he principally has in mind the reconciling of human beings to God. But the disciple who composed the letter to the Ephesians in his name extended the image to the 'horizontal' plane as well: Christ has worked reconciliation between human beings themselves.[7] A key passage of the letter (2:13-16) recalls the barrier or fence in the Temple in Jerusalem separating the court of the Jews from that of the Gentiles. As no Gentile was allowed through that barrier under pain of death, nothing could symbolise more potently the rigid separation between the two. For the 'Paul' who speaks in Ephesians, Christ has smashed down that divisive barrier, creating out of the two peoples a single humanity modelled upon the pattern of his own risen state. So that there are no longer 'aliens or foreign visitors' in the household of God, no second-class citizens. All are 'citizens' and 'saints', all are being 'built into a single house where God dwells in the Spirit' (vv. 19-22).

The vision presented here looks primarily, of course, to the union of Jew and Gentile in the Christian Church. But there are hints in Ephesians of a still more extensive reconciliation. The mighty work of reconciling Jew and Gentile in the Church is simply a token or pledge of what God's power can yet achieve on a more universal, even cosmic, scale (1:9-10, 18-23; 3:16-21).

The upshot would appear to be that wherever human communities stand in need of reconciliation, there, within this vision, is scope for the continuance of God's costly redemptive work. The task before Aboriginal and other inhabitants of Australia sits well within the perspective of this Pauline view of reconciliation still to be made complete in Christ.

Hebrews

We began this biblical reflection upon reconciliation recalling the motif of the quest for a promised land. No New Testament document evokes this theme so powerfully as the Letter to the Hebrews. For the (unknown) author of this work the Christian life is essentially a re-enactment of the desert wandering of the ancient people of God. On earth Christians have no 'abiding city' (15:14) in which to dwell. Their life is guided by faith in the reality of a future which they cannot see but which they hope to reach (11:1). Like their spiritual ancestors they can describe themselves as 'strangers and nomads on earth', people 'in search of their real homeland' (11:14)—ever pressing on.

The hope that finds expression here can be focused upon a purely other-worldly future—and that has been a traditional interpretation. But it is also possible to see such a future in a way more continuous with the current life on earth. In this view, what is hoped for is a dimension of our present possession of our land, one in which spiritual and transcendent values will be paramount and justice reign supreme.

We can settle for the present physical possession which we have and seek to enjoy as best we may the material rewards it provides. But the hope emerging from Hebrews, of a 'city with foundations, designed and built by God' (11:10), suggests a deeper, richer possession—one where spirit has pride of place, where greed and exploitation are alien and where all find common ground.

The original inhabitants of this land have a spiritual vision of it, one which two centuries of dispossession have not managed to suppress. The land will become for all the 'promised land' when other Australians respect and share the insights and values they have held for millennia in trust. Reverence for the spirit in all its manifestations will be a key aspect of the total process.

Conclusion

This paper has considered the challenge facing us Australians in the light of several New Testament presentations of the Christian gospel. Rather than attempt to distil a single unified picture from all—a tour de force at best—I have tried to show the particular light each might shed upon the task before us. I have, however, sought to throw a unifying bracket around the whole by opening and closing with the idea of 'homecoming', 'possession of the promised land'. Beneath this, I believe, lies the hope for genuinely Australian spirituality—something which the contemporary prophetic writers Patrick White and Manning Clark reminded us, before their recent deaths, Australia needs before all else. No genuine spirituality can rest upon injustice or denial of the historic truth. The proposed process of reconciliation is part of our own home-coming to this land and to the centre of ourselves.

Appendix 1

Pope John Paul II speaks to Aborigines

Alice Springs, 29 November 1986

'The hour of hope has come'

It is a great joy for me to be here today in Alice Springs and to meet so many of you, the Aborigines and Torres Strait Islanders of Australia. I want to tell you right away how much the Church esteems and loves you, and how much she wishes to assist you in your spiritual and material needs.

At the beginning of time, as God's Spirit moved over the waters, he began to communicate something of his goodness and beauty to all Creation.

When God then created men and women, he gave them the good things of the Earth for their use and benefit; and he put into their hearts abilities and powers, which were his gifts. And to all human beings throughout the ages God has given a desire for himself, a desire which different cultures have tried to express in their own ways.

As the human family spread over the face of the Earth, your people settled and lived in this big country that stood apart from all the others. Other people did not even know this land was here; they only knew that somewhere in the southern oceans of the world there was 'The Great South Land of the Holy Spirit'.

But for thousands of years you have lived in this land

and fashioned a culture that endures to this day. And during all this time, the Spirit of God has been with you. Your Dreaming, which influences your lives so strongly that, no matter what happens, you remain forever people of your culture, is your own way of touching the mystery of God's spirit in you and in Creation. You must keep your striving for God and hold on to it in your lives.

The rock paintings and the discovered evidence of your ancient tools and implements indicate the presence of your age-old culture of this land.

Your culture must not be allowed to disappear

Your culture, which shows the lasting genius and dignity of your race, must not be allowed to disappear.

Do not think that your gifts are worth so little that you should no longer bother to maintain them. Share them with each other and teach them to your children. Your songs, your stories, your paintings, your dances, your languages must never be lost.

Do you, perhaps, remember those words that Paul VI spoke to the Aboriginal people during his visit to them in 1970? On that occasion he said: 'We know that you have a lifestyle proper to your own ethnic genius of culture—a culture which the Church respects and which she does not in any way ask you to renounce. Society itself is enriched by the presence of different cultural and ethnic elements.

'For us, you and the values you represent are precious. We deeply respect your dignity and reiterate our deep affection for you' (Sydney, 2 December 1970).

For thousands of years this culture of yours was free to grow without interference by people from other places. You lived your lives in spiritual closeness to the land, with its animals, birds, fishes, waterholes, rivers, hills and mountains.

Through your closeness to the land you touched the sacredness of man's relationship with God, for the land was the proof of a power in life greater than yourselves. You did not spoil the land, use it up, exhaust it, and then walk away from it. You realised that your land was related to the source of life.

The silence of the Bush taught you a quietness of soul that put you in touch with another world, the world of God's Spirit. Your careful attention to the details of kinship spoke of your reverence for birth, life and human generation. You knew that children need to be loved, to be full of joy. They need a time to grow in laughter and to play, secure in the knowledge that they belong to their people.

Respect for law

You had a great respect for the need which people have for law, as a guide to living fairly with each other. So you created a legal system—very strict it is true but closely adapted to the country in which you lived your lives. It made your society orderly. It was one of the reasons why you survived in this land.

You marked the growth of young men and women with ceremonies of discipline that taught them responsibility as they came to maturity.

These achievements are indications of human strivings. And in these strivings you showed a dignity open to the message of God's revealed wisdom to all men and women, which is the great truth of the Gospel of Jesus Christ.

Some of the stories from your Dreamtime legends speak powerfully of the great mysteries of human life, its frailty, its need for help, its closeness to spiritual powers and the value of the human person. They are not unlike some of the great inspired lessons from the people among whom Jesus was born.

It is wonderful to see how people, as they accept the Gospel of Jesus, find points of agreement between their own traditions and those of Jesus and his people.

You have endured the flames

The culture which this long and careful growth produced was

not prepared for the sudden meeting with another people, with different customs and traditions, who came to your country nearly two hundred years ago. They were different from Aboriginal people. Their traditions, the organisation of their lives, and their attitudes to the land were quite strange to you.

Their law, too, was quite different. These people had knowledge, money and power; and they brought with them some patterns of behaviour from which the Aboriginal people were unable to protect themselves.

The effects of some of those forces are still active among you today. Many of you have been dispossessed of your traditional lands, and separated from your tribal ways, though some of you still have your traditional culture. Some of you are establishing Aboriginal communities in the towns and cities.

For others there is still no real place for camp-fires and kinship observances except on the fringes of country towns. There, work is hard to find, and education in a different cultural background is difficult. The discrimination caused by racism is a daily experience.

You have learned how to survive, whether on your own lands, or scattered among the towns and cities. Though your difficulties are not yet over, you must draw on the endurance which your ancient ceremonies have taught you. Endurance brings with it patience; patience helps you to find the way ahead, and gives you courage for your journey.

Take heart from the fact that many of your languages are still spoken and that you still possess your ancient culture. You have kept your sense of brotherhood. If you stay closely united, you are like a tree standing in the middle of a bush-fire sweeping through the timber. The leaves are scorched and the tough bark is scarred and burned; but inside the tree the *sap is still flowing*, and under the ground the roots are still strong. Like that tree you have endured the flames, and you still have the power to be reborn.

The time for this rebirth is now!

Some have loved and cared for you

We know that during the last two hundred years certain people tried to understand you, to learn about you, to respect your ways and to honour you as persons. These men and women, as you soon realised, were different from others of their race. They loved and cared for the indigenous people.

They began to share with you their stories of God, helped you cope with sickness, tried to protect you from ill-treatment. They were honest with you, and showed you by their lives how they tried to avoid the bad things in their own culture. These people were not always successful, and there were times when they did not fully understand you.

But they showed you goodwill and friendship. They came from many different walks of life. Some were teachers and doctors and other professional people; some were simple folk. History will remember the good example of their charity and fraternal solidarity.

Among those who have loved and cared for the indigenous people, we especially recall with profound gratitude all the missionaries of the Christian faith. With immense generosity they gave their lives in service to you and to your forebears. They helped to educate the Aboriginal people and offered health and social services.

Whatever their human frailty, and whatever mistakes they may have made, nothing can ever minimise the depth of their charity. Nothing can ever cancel out their greatest contribution, which was to proclaim to you Jesus Christ and to establish his Church in your midst.

The Church still supports you today

From the earliest times, men like Archbishop Polding of Sydney opposed the legal fiction adopted by European settlers that this land was *terra nullius*—nobody's country. He strongly pleaded for the rights of the Aboriginal inhabitants to keep the traditional lands on which their whole society depended. The Church still supports you today.

Let it not be said that the fair and equitable recognition of Aboriginal rights to land is discrimination. To call for the acknowledgment of the land rights of people who have never surrendered those rights is not discrimination. Certainly, what has been done cannot be undone. But what can now be done to remedy the deeds of yesterday must not be put off till tomorrow.

Christian people of goodwill are saddened to realise— many of them only recently—for how long a time Aboriginal people were transported from their homelands into small areas or reserves where families were broken up, tribes split apart, children orphaned and people forced to live like exiles in a foreign country.

The reserves still exist today, and require a just and proper settlement that still lies unachieved. The urban problems resulting from the transportation and separation of people still have to be addressed, so that these people may make a new start in life with each other once again.

The establishment of a new society for Aboriginal people cannot go forward without just and mutually recognised agreements with regard to these human problems, even though their causes lie in the past. The greatest value to be achieved by such agreements, which must be implemented without causing new injustices, is respect for the dignity and growth of the human person.

And you, the Aboriginal people of this country and its cities, must show that you are actively working for your own dignity of life. On your part, you must show that you too can walk tall and command the respect which every human being expects to receive from the rest of the human family.

The Gospel esteems and embraces all cultures

The Gospel of our Lord Jesus Christ speaks all languages, it esteems and embraces all cultures. It supports them in everything human and, when necessary, it purifies them. Always and everywhere the Gospel uplifts and enriches cultures with the revealed message of a loving and merciful God.

That Gospel now invites you to become, through and through, Aboriginal Christians. It meets your deepest desires. You do not have to be people divided into two parts, as though an Aboriginal had to borrow the faith and life of Christianity, like a hat or a pair of shoes, from someone else who owns them. Jesus calls you to accept his words and his values into your own culture. To develop in this way will make you more than ever truly Aboriginal.

The old ways can draw new life and strength from the Gospel. The message of Jesus Christ can lift up your lives to new heights, reinforce all your positive values and add many others, which only the Gospel in its originality proposes. Take this Gospel into your own language and way of speaking; let its spirit penetrate your communities and determine your behaviour towards each other, let it bring new strength to your stories and your ceremonies.

Let the Gospel come into your hearts and renew your personal lives. The Church invites you to express the living word of Jesus in ways that speak to your Aboriginal minds and hearts. All over the world people worship God and read his word in their own language, and colour the great signs and symbols of religion with touches of their own traditions. Why should you be different from them in this regard, why should you not be allowed the happiness of being with God and each other in Aboriginal fashion?

As you listen to the Gospel of our Lord Jesus Christ, seek out the best things of your traditional ways. If you do, you will come to realise more and more your great human and Christian dignity. Let your minds and hearts be strengthened to begin a new life now.

A time for new courage and new hope

Past hurts cannot be healed by violence, nor are present injustices removed by resentment. Your Christian faith calls you to become the best kind of Aboriginal people you can be. This is possible only if reconciliation and forgiveness are part of your lives.

Only then will you find happiness. Only then will you make your best contribution to all your brothers and sisters in this great nation. You are part of Australia and Australia is part of you. And the Church herself in Australia will not be fully the Church that Jesus wants her to be until you have made your contribution to her life and until that contribution has been joyfully received by others.

In the new world that is emerging for you, you are being called to live fully human and Christian lives, not to die of shame and sorrow. But you know that to fulfil your role you need a new heart. You will already feel courage rise up inside you when you listen to God speaking to you in these words of the prophets:

'Do not be afraid for I have redeemed you; I have called you by your name, you are mine. Do not be afraid for I am with you.' (Isaiah 43:1, 5).

And again:

'I am going to ... gather you together ... and bring you home to your own land ... I shall give you a new heart and put a new spirit in you ... You shall be my people and I will be your God' (Ezekiel 36:24, 26, 28).

With you I rejoice in the hope of God's gift of salvation, which has its beginnings here and now, and which also depends on how we behave towards each other, on what we do, on how we honour God and love all people.

Dear Aboriginal people: the hour has come for you to take on new courage and new hope. You are called to remember the past, to be faithful to your worthy traditions, and to adapt your living culture whenever this is required by your own needs and those of your fellow man. Above all you are called to open your hearts evermore to the consoling, purifying and uplifting message of Jesus Christ, the son of God, who died so that we might all have life, and have it to the full (see John 10:10).

Appendix 2

Pastoral Letter of the Australian Catholic Bishops to the Catholic People of Australia

ABORIGINAL SUNDAY 1990

Sharing the country through understanding

When Aborigines met with Pope John Paul II in Alice Springs, they prayed to the Father of us all:

> We ask you to help the people of Australia to listen to us and respect our culture. Make the knowledge of you grow strong in all people, so that you can be at home in us and we can make a home for everyone in our Land.

At Alice Springs, the Pope challenged us all when he said to Aborigines:

> The Church herself in Australia will not be fully the Church that Jesus wants her to be until you have made your contribution of her life and until that contribution has been joyfully received by others.

It is appropriate that as a Church we recognise the past and present injustices suffered by Aborigines and we reflect on the need for national reconciliation today and how each of us may contribute to one another's right to belong in Australian society. Hearing Paul's words to the Romans (Romans 12:2) we do so not by modelling ourselves on the behaviour of the world around us, but by letting our attitude and behaviour change, being modelled on a new way of seeing the world, through the eyes of Jesus. To do this, we have to renounce ourselves and take up our cross, following the footsteps of Jesus (Matthew 16:21-27).

For some years, there has been talk about an Aboriginal treaty in Australia. Many Aboriginal leaders have said that there is a need for some legal document which recognises the dispossession suffered by Aborigines and Torres Strait Islanders in the past and which guarantees them a place of belonging in Australia now and in the future. Other people have argued that the past is past and all that needs to be done is to treat all Australians the same.

Reconciliation

The Prime Minister, Mr Hawke, sees the needs for an instrument of reconciliation as the outcome of consultations which will succeed only with the support of the majority of Australians. The Leader of the Opposition, Dr Hewson, recognising the importance of reconciliation, has said that there may be room for considerable common ground between the major political parties on this issue.

There has been a lot of misunderstanding about the word 'treaty'. Our parliamentarians would prefer another word while many Aboriginal leaders want to keep the word 'treaty'.

As we know from all the statistics we hear, Aborigines are still very badly off, often living on the fringes of society.

Grim reminder

The reports of the Royal Commission into Aboriginal Deaths in Custody have been a grim reminder to us all that many Australian Aborigines are marginalised.

To belong in our society, Aborigines are entitled to preserve their cultural identity, while remaining open to others. Aborigines should not be forced to assimilate. That would be like forcing people to be migrants, becoming part of a foreign culture against their will.

Having the right to maintain their identity, Aborigines should have the opportunity to choose their lifestyle. If they integrate into the surrounding society, it should be as a free choice.

Realistic alternatives

Aborigines must be guaranteed realistic alternatives, when seeking social and political organisation.

We have to move beyond the simple idea that assimilation is the answer.

Equality is not the same as uniformity. In its recent document *The Church and Racism*, the Pontifical Commission for Justice and Peace has said:

> Equality of treatment ... implies a certain recognition of differences which minorities themselves demand in order to develop according to their own specific characteristics, in respect for others and for the common good of society and the world community.

Respect for each other's differences can challenge our simple Australian ideas about equality and a fair go for everyone. Even in Church life we have to face questions like: 'Why can't they just be like the rest of us? We have our parish structures, why won't they participate?'

We need to be educated to a positive appreciation of the complementary diversity of others. It is not racist to respect the special position and needs of others.

Aborigines are not just one group among many in the community who are in need of welfare assistance. One Aboriginal leader has said: 'We are not just poor whites. No policy should proceed on that basis'.

As descendants of Australia's first occupants and as the primary custodians of the Aboriginal culture and heritage, Aborigines have a right to continue the management of their community affairs as autonomously as possible within the Australian nation provided they do not act contrary to the common good nor interfere with the rights of others, and provided all community members are given a realistic choice between their community life and lifestyles available to other Australians.

At Alice Springs, the Pope said there was a need for 'a just and proper settlement that still lives unachieved' in this country. He went on to say:

> The establishment of a new society for Aboriginal people cannot go forward without just and mutually recognised agreements with regard to these human problems, even though their causes lie in the past. The greatest value to be achieved by such agreements, which must be implemented without causing new injustices, is respect for the dignity and growth of the human person.

During the bicentenary, we issued a pastoral letter in which we asked all governments to encourage Aboriginal self-management and independence, to involve Aborigines in all decisions that affect them, and to recognise in practical ways that Australia at the time of European settlement was not *terra nullius* (nobody's country). We saw a role for everyone, including governments, in a task of national reconciliation.

In January 1988, Cardinal Clancy, as President of the Australian Catholic Bishops' Conference, joined with 13 other church leaders in a statement entitled, *Towards Reconciliation in Australian Society*. They set out four requirements for a just and proper settlement:

1. A secure land base for dispossessed Aboriginal communities with special attention being given to traditional communities on their lands, family groups on pastoral properties and fringe dwellers outside country towns.

2. A just process for the resolution of conflicting claims to the land and its use, especially between Aborigines, pastoralists and miners.

3. An assured place for powerless Aborigines in our political

processes with provision for Aboriginal councils at local, state and federal levels.

4. A guaranteed future for Aboriginal culture and tradition with legal protection of Aboriginal heritage, and public education of all Australians about Aboriginal history and the vitality of contemporary Aboriginal culture.

They asked that the Federal Parliament make formal acknowledgment of the nation's Aboriginal prehistory and the enduring place of our Aboriginal heritage. Many Australians had hoped this could be done by the passage of a suitable resolution with unanimous support as the first item of substantive business in the new Parliament House. The resolution was passed but unfortunately it was not unanimous.

We hope that the renewed efforts by the Prime Minister and the Leader of the Opposition for bipartisan agreement on the process of reconciliation will bear fruit. In addition to well resourced and properly targeted welfare, education and training programs, there is still a need for formal acknowledgment of the special place of Aborigines in Australian society. Hopefully the debate about the word 'treaty' will stop us from finding how best to express the assured place of Aboriginal culture and heritage in the Australian nation.

A good lesson for us all

The year 1988 was a good lesson for us all. We did not know how to speak about ourselves as a nation according Aborigines their due place. We learnt that white Australia has a black history. The next symbolic moment in Australian history is 1 January 2001, the first centenary of the Australian Constitution. There is time to act, but we must start now. The treaty (or whatever it is to be called) cannot be resolved overnight by the Commonwealth Government and a group of Aboriginal leaders. All levels of government must be involved. Local Aboriginal communities must be part of the process. The community generally must be involved, not simply as spectators waiting to be presented with a final document. We who are the Church must play our role as reconcilers whether we are Aboriginal or non-Aboriginal Australians.

The character of the Australian nation has been shaped by our history. There was no agreement negotiated between Aborigines and British authorities. Soldiers, convicts and 'free settlers' drove Aborigines away from their lands. Colonists disregarded British instructions given to Captain Cook to take possession of land 'with the consent of the natives'. As a result, Australian laws have remained flawed and underdeveloped for over two hundred years. Since the 1967 referendum when the great majority of Australian showed support for Aborigines, our Commonwealth and State Parliaments have taken steps to recognise some Aboriginal land rights and to give Aborigines better opportunity to participate and manage their own affairs. It is for Aboriginal representatives, lawyers and politicians to work out how our legal system can be improved so that rights of Aborigines are better protected and so they can be assured a place of belonging. We will not do this by denying the facts of history nor by using political rhetoric which in no way matches our intentions or commitment. If we start now, we should be able to reach a just and proper settlement by 2001. There should be a new beginning in living together in this land.

'So all of us have to live together ...'

When the Prime Minister promised Aborigines a treaty at Barunga, Northern Territory, in 1988, one of the elders, Mr Wenten Rubuntja said:

> Today there are a lot of people living in this country. People who have come from all over the world. But we don't call them foreigners. We don't ask 'Where's your country? Where's your father from?' They have been born here. Their mother's blood is in the country ... This is their country too now.
>
> So all of us have to live together. We have to look after each other. We have to share this country. And this means respecting each other's laws and cultures. We have to work out a way of

108 Reconciling Our Differences

sharing this country, but there has to be an understanding of and respect of our culture, our law. Hopefully that's what this treaty will mean.

Whatever the final document is called, it should help us to show more understanding and respect for each other so that we can share this land in which all may belong. Celebrating the 150th anniversary of the Treaty of Waitangi our brother bishops in New Zealand asked their Church members to be 'constructive builders of structures of harmony and grace'.

Together, as God's instruments of reconciliation, we still need to hear the Lord's promise communicated through the prophet Ezekiel:

I am going to gather you together and bring you home to your own land. I shall give you a new heart and put a new spirit in you. You shall be my people and I will be your God (Ezekiel 30:24, 26, 28).

No Australian need be alien to the land or to the society which is the common heritage of all, from the Aborigine to the newest migrant.

For all to belong, we need 'a just and proper settlement'.

Wouldn't it be good if every Australian could proudly call this land 'My Place'?

Notes to the Chapters

Introduction

1. F. Brennan, J. Egan and J. Honner, *Finding Common Ground*, Dove Communications, 1st edition, 1985; and F. Brennan, W. Daniel, J. Egan and J. Honner, *Finding Common Ground*, Collins Dove, 2nd edition, 1986.

Chapter 1

1. Barbara Tuchman, in *Practising History*, London, 1982, p. 18.
2. John 8:32.
3. Henry Reynolds, *Frontier*, Sydney, 1987, p. 195.
4. Peter Biskup, in G. Osborne and W.F. Mandle (eds), *New History*, Sydney, 1982, p. 14; J. Molony, *History of Australia*, Melbourne, 1987, pp. ix, x.
5. See also Robert Reece 'The Aborigines and Australian Historiography', in J.A. Moses (ed.), *Historical Disciplines and Culture in Australia*, Brisbane, 1979.
6. D.J. Mulvaney and J. H. Callaby, *'So Much That is New': Baldwin Spencer 1860-1929*, Melbourne, 1985.
7. C.D. Rowley, *Aboriginal Policy and Practice*, 3 vols, Canberra, 1970-1. See also for examples of work readily available G. Bolton, *Spoils and Spoilers*, Sydney, 1981; N. Butlin, *Close Encounters of the Worst Kind*, Canberra, 1982; G. Blainey, *Triumph of the Nomads*, Melbourne, 1975 and *A Land Half Won*, Melbourne, 1980; R. Broome *Aboriginal Austral-*

ians: Black Response to White Dominance, Sydney, 1982; and the magnificent general and specialist work of W.E.H. Stanner and Dianne Barwick.

8. For recent debates about the convicts, see S. Nicholas, *Convict Workers; Reinterpreting Australia's Past*, Melbourne, 1988, and e.g. Robert Hughes, *The Fatal Shore*, Sydney, 1987.

9. Frank Brennan uses the analogy of ink, and quotes from Stanner in *Finding Common Ground*, Melbourne, 1986, pp. 12-13.

10. J. Peter White, in *Australians to 1788*, Sydney, 1987, ch. 5; N. Butlin, *Our Original Aggression*, Canberra, 1982; H. Reynolds, *Frontier*, passim.

11. Bain Attwood, *The Making of the Aborigines*, Sydney, 1989.

12. Noel Butlin, *The Great Australian Take-Over*, Canberra, unpub, ms., 1990.

13. V. Rae Ellis, *Black Robinson: Protector of Aborigines*, Melbourne, 1988.

14. H. Reynolds, *With the White People*, Sydney, 1990; John Harris, *One Blood: 200 years of Aboriginal Encounter with Christianity*, Sydney, 1990; see also on the 'second onslaught' Bain Attwood, op. cit.

15. 'James Stephen and Colonial Policy', in *The Journal of Imperial and Commonwealth History*, Jan 1992, pp. 21ff.

16. H. Reynolds, *The Law of the Land*, Sydney, 1987.

17. Frank Brennan, *Sharing the Country*, Melbourne, Penguin, 1992, pp. 25, 31.

18. ibid., pp. 43f, 148.

19. Stanner in *After the Dreaming*, Sydney, 1969, p. 25. On regional and sectional topics there are many books and articles. Some examples are M.F. Christie, *Aborigines in Colonial Victoria*, Sydney 1979; L. Ryan, *The Aboriginal Tasmanians*, Brisbane, 1981; F. Brennan, *Land Rights, Queensland Style*, Brisbane 1992; A. Allingham, *Taming the Wilderness*, Townsville, 1977; Ray Evans, Kay Saunders and Kathryn Cronin (eds), *Race Relations in Colonial Queensland: A History of Exclusion, Exploitation and Extermination*, Brisbane 1975; Clive Turnbull, *Black War: the extermination of the Tasmanian Aborigines*, Melbourne, 1948; Lorna Lippmann, *Generations of Resistance*, Sydney, 1981; L.L. Robson, *A History of Tasmania*, Vol 1, Melbourne, 1983; John Summers, chs 11 and 18 in E. Richards (ed.), *The Flinders History of South Australia*, Adelaide, 1986; C.T. Stannage (ed.), *A New History of Western Australia*, Perth, 1981.

20. For example, A.T. Yarwood and M.J. Knowling, *Race Relations in Australia*, Sydney, 1982.

21. For example, M. Roe, *The Quest for Authority in Eastern Australia, 1835-51*, Melbourne 1965; A. Markus, *Governing Savages*, Sydney, 1990, who goes some way to lighten the unrelieved picture of doom, and

describes in detail at least one series of attempts at 'conciling', with portraits of the 'types' involved; Ian Donaldson and Tamsin Donaldson (eds), *Seeing the First Australians*, Sydney 1985, which successfully shows how power relationships affected mutual recognition, and goes far to hinting how a re-imagined Australia might find Aboriginal perspectives most valuable.

22. Broome, op. cit., p. 119.
23. Hancock, *Today, Yesterday and Tomorrow*, Boyer Lectures 1973; Lines, *Taming the Wilderness*, Sydney, 1991, pp. 13, 81, and Trollope, at p. 115.
24. D.J. Mulvaney and J. Peter White, in *Australians to 1788*, in *Australians: A Historical Library*, Sydney 1987; V. Burgmann and J. Lee (eds), *A People's History of Australia*, Sydney, 1988, vol. 1, ch. 1; R. Ward, *Finding Australia*, Sydney, 1987.
25. J.J. Eddy, 'What are the Origins of Australia's National Identity', in F.G. Castles (ed.), *Australia Compared*, Sydney, pp. 17f; C.M.H. Clark, *A Discovery of Australia*, Boyer Lectures, 1976, pp. 23, 47.
26. A. McGrath, 'Europeans and Aborigines', in N. Meaney (ed.), *Under New Heavens*, Sydney, 1989.

Chapter 2

1. Donald N. Larson, *Not All Humans Are People*, CMS Publishing Inc, Minnesota, 1986.
2. Commissioner Muirhead released an *Interim Report* of the Royal Commission into Aboriginal Deaths in Custody [RCIADIC] in 1988, around the same time that Western Australia released an *Interim Inquiry* by Philip Vincent. In 1991 the final *National Report* was completed. It consisted of five volumes and accompanying it were various *Regional Reports of Inquiry into Individual Deaths in Custody*. There was a *Regional Report* for Western Australia and one for Queensland. There was a combined *Regional Report* for Victoria, New South Wales and Tasmania. In addition there was a two volume *Regional Report of Inquiry into Underlying Issues in Western Australia* by Commissioner Dodson. And there were 99 individual *Reports of Inquiry* into each of the deaths, some of which, as in the case of John Pat, were quite lengthy.
3. J.H. Wootten, *RCIADIC, Regional Report of Inquiry in New South Wales, Victoria and Tasmania*, Australian Government Publishing Service, Canberra, 1991, p. 21.
4. ibid., p. 21.
5. ibid., p. 11.

112   Reconciling Our Differences

6. D.J. O'Dea, *RCIADIC, Regional Report of Inquiry into Individual Deaths in Custody in Western Australia*, Australian Government Publishing Service, volume 1, pp. 171f.
7. ibid., p. 171.
8. ibid., p. 152.
9. E. Johnston, *RCIADIC, Report of the Inquiry into the Death of John Peter Pat*, Australian Government Publishing Service, Canberra, 1991, p. 2.
10. ibid., p. 15.
11. ibid., p. 18.
12. ibid., p. 21.
13. ibid., p. 12.
14. It now appears somewhat instructive, and tragic, that the name given to this largely Aboriginal town, Roebourne, was the name of Western Australia's first surveyor-general.
15. ibid., p. 279.
16. ibid., p. 279.
17. In 1965, Hammersley Iron and the construction of the port and town of Dampier; 1968, town of Karratha; 1970, Robe River, Pannawonica, port of Cape Lambert and town of Wickham. In 1980 there also began the Northwest Shelf Natural Gas Development Project.
18. ibid., p. 249. Mr Brian Bull, presently the WA Commissioner for Police, had at that time been appointed as Chief Superintendent (Discipline).
19. E. Johnston, *RCIADIC, National Report*, Australian Government Publishing Service, volume 2, p. 131.
20. ANOP Market Research—Government and Industry, *Land Rights, Winning Middle Australia, An Attitude and Communications Research Study*, Crows Nest, 1985, p. 1.
21. ibid., p. 14.
22. P.L. Dodson, *RCIADIC, Regional Report of Inquiry into Underlying Issues in Western Australia*, Australian Government Publishing Service, Canberra, 1991, p. 224.
23. J.H. Wootten, op. cit., p. 187.
24. E. Johnston, op. cit., volume 2, p. 157.
25. *The West Australian*, Saturday 14 March 1992.
26. P.L. Dodson, op. cit., p. 711.
27. ibid., p. 729.
28. ANOP Market Research, op. cit., p. 5.
29. E. Johnston, op. cit., volume 2, pp. 155, 156.
30. J.H. Wootten, op. cit., p. 11.
31. P.L. Dodson, op. cit., p. 766.
32. J.H. Wootten, op. cit., p. 148.
33. P.L. Dodson, op. cit., p. 766.

34. E. Johnston, op. cit., volume 1, p. 102.
35. ibid., p. 112.
36. ibid., p. 112.
37. J.H. Wootten, op. cit., p. 88.
38. E. Johnston, op. cit., volume 1, p. 70.
39. ibid., p. 77.
40. ibid., p. 79.
41. ibid., p. 81.
42. ibid., p. 81.
43. Commissioner O'Dea writes: 'One cannot be impressed with these crude, if not callous, means which were used to clean up an unconscious human being ...' *RCIADIC, Report of the Inquiry into the Death of Albert Dougal*, Australian Government Publishing Service, Canberra, 1989, p. 12.
44. D.J. O'Dea, ibid., p. 20.
45. J.H. Wootten, op. cit., p. 17.
46. Police were given the role of 'policing' the frontier in remote parts of Australia, a role which the military performed in other countries, e.g. North America. They also led punitive expeditions which often were massacres.
47. ibid., p. 300.
48. The Commission research also found that Aboriginal people tend to be held in custody longer than non-Aboriginal people in remote areas of Australia. See *National Report*, volume 3, p. 22.
49. J.H. Wootten, op. cit., p. 289.
50. ibid., p. 291.
51. E. Johnston, op. cit., volume 3, p. 6.
52. E. Johnston, op. cit., volume 5, p. 58.
53. It is significant, in terms of the theme of this paper, that while the overall support for the referendum by non-Aboriginal people was extremely high, where it was low was where non-Aboriginal people lived in closer contact with Aboriginal people.
54. P.L. Dodson, op. cit., p. 35.
55. E. Johnston, op. cit., volume 5, p. 65.
56. E. Johnston, op. cit., volume 5, p. 69.
57. ibid., p. 65.
58. ibid., p. 65.
59. ibid., p. 65.
60. *The West Australian*, Friday 10 May 1991.
61. *The West Australian*, Monday 13 May 1991.
62. *The West Australian*, Tuesday 14 May 1991.
63. *The West Australian*, Wednesday 8 May 1991.
64. *The West Australian*, Saturday 7 May 1991.

Chapter 3

1. R. Hawke to J. Hewson, 7 May 1990.
2. J. Hewson to R. Hawke, 22 June 1990.
3. P.L. Dodson, 'Duty of Care', *Australian Left Review,* September 1991, p. 28.
4. *Sydney Morning Herald,* 18 August 1989.
5. (1985) 298 *QPD* 4741.
6. (1982) 287 *QPD* 5172.
7. *The Age,* 2 April 1992.
8. Saulwick Poll, 16-17 March 1992.
9. Department of Foreign Affairs and Trade, Memorandum, 929/34/10/5, 14 January 1992.
10. Department of Foreign Affairs and Trade, Statement to the United Nations Association of Australia Conference 1991.

Chapter 4

1. Cited in Frank Brennan, 'Aboriginal self-determination: The "new partnership" of the 1990s', *Alternative Law Journal* 17 (1992) 54.
2. Quoted by Frank Brennan, art. cit., p. 54.
3. Howard McGary, 'Groups, Moral Status of', in L.C. Becker & B.C. Becker (eds), *Encyclopedia of Ethics,* New York, Garland, 1992, p. 425.
4. David Hollenbach, *Claims in Conflict,* New York, Paulist, 1979, p. 7.
5. ibid., ch. 3, 'A Christian Theory of Rights?'.
6. See above, footnote 2.
7. Frank Brennan, *Sharing the Country,* Melbourne, Penguin, 1992, p. 22.
8. ibid., pp. 44f.

Chapter 5—A Brief Bibliography

Attwood, B., *The Making of the Aborigines,* Allen and Unwin, Sydney, 1989.
Berndt, R.M. & Berndt, C.H., *The World of the First Australians,* Aboriginal Studies Press, Canberra, 1988.
Boff, L., *Liberating Grace,* Orbis, Maryknoll NY, 1979.
Elder, B., *Blood on the Wattle,* Child and Associates, Sydney, 1988.
Niebuhr, H.R., *Christ and Culture,* Harper & Row, New York, 1975.

Sobrino, J., *The True Church and the Poor*, Orbis, New York, 1984.

Vatican II Documents, e.g. as edited by W.M. Abbott, *The Documents of Vatican II*, Geoffrey Chapman, London – Dublin, 1966.

Worms, E.A., *Australian Aboriginal Religions*, Nelen Yubu, 1986.

Chapter 6

1. In historical reality the Israelite conquest may have been more gradual, more the result of assimilation than outright military action. Moreover, the central theme of Joshua is not military conquest as such but the truth that the land is entirely the gift of God and that its tenure depends upon obedience to the divine will; see A.F. Campbell, *The Study Companion to Old Testament Literature*, Wilmington, Glazier, 1989, pp. 169-70, 181-82.

2. See M. D. Coogan, 'Joshua' in *New Jerome Biblical Commentary*, Englewood Cliffs, NJ, Prentice Hall, 1990, pp. 110-31; see pp. 111-12 (§ 8).

3. For an impressive, though in many respects flawed, example of an approach along these lines, see C. Myers, *Binding the Strong Man: a Political Reading of Mark's Story of Jesus*, New York, Orbis, 1988; see esp. pp. 13-14.

4. See J.A. Fitzmyer, *The Gospel according to Luke X-XXIV*, New York, Doubleday, 1985, pp. 1220-22.

5. See C.H. Dodd, *The Interpretation of the Fourth Gospel*, Cambridge, Cambridge University, 1953, p. 263.

6. For this symbolic view of the Lazarus miracle see B. Byrne, *Lazarus: A Contemporary Reading of the Fourth Gospel*, Homebush, St. Paul Publications, 1991.

7. For the 'reconciliation' theme in Ephesians see R.P. Martin, *Reconciliation: A Study of Paul's Theology*, Atlanta, John Knox, 1980, pp. 157-98.

Contributors

Brendan Byrne SJ teaches New Testament at the United Faculty of Theology, Melbourne, and has written extensively in New Testament criticism and commentary. He is a member of the Pontifical Biblical Commission.

Frank Brennan SJ is Director of Uniya, a social research and action agency sponsored by the Australian Jesuits. He has been involved with Aboriginal communities and issues for over ten years and is author of the recently published *Sharing the Country* (Penguin 1992) and *Land Rights Queensland Style* (UQP 1992).

William Daniel SJ is a moral theologian who teaches at the United Faculty of Theology. He has written widely on moral questions, including issues of Aboriginal rights. He was a member of the Fraser government's Uranium Advisory Council.

J.J. Eddy SJ is Senior Research Fellow in History at the Research School of Social Sciences, Australian National University. He has written widely on Australian and imperial history and government, and in 1992-93 convenes a course at the ANU on the history of Australian immigration.

Brian McCoy SJ has worked among Aborigines for over twenty years. He was employed as a researcher for the Royal Commission into Black Deaths in Custody and was based in Broome, WA for the task. He is currently living among the Kukatja-speaking people at Balgo, WA.

John Wilcken SJ is a systematic theologian who teaches at the United Faculty of Theology. He has written on a wide range of theological and spiritual subjects and is currently superior of Corpus Christi Community, Greenvale, Victoria.